BOMI Institute's Leasing Reference Guide

The Practical Guide to Lease Development
The Practical Guide to Lease Negotiation
The Practical Guide to Lease Administration

Financial Series

BUILDING OWNERS AND MANAGERS INSTITUTE

Printed in the United States of America

ISBN: 1-928594-91-3

Disclaimer

This publication is designed to serve as an educational tool in regard to the subject matter covered. It is sold and distributed with the understanding that the publisher is not engaged in rendering legal, accounting, real estate, or other professional services. If such services are required, the services of competent professionals should be sought with respect to particular matters in question.

The reader should not rely on this publication for the resolution of specific questions that apply to a particular set of facts. In addition, the publishers, authors, and editors assume no liability of any kind whatsoever resulting from the use of or reliance upon the contents of this course material.

Contents

Publisher's Acknowledgments

BOMI would like to thank Sarah Nettles, a subject matter expert who reviewed the content of this Reference Guide and provided critical feedback. Ms. Nettles, RPA, is a Building Manager for Carter, headquartered in Atlanta, Georgia. Carter is Atlanta's oldest and largest privately-held full-service commercial real estate firm, providing property management, development, transaction, and investment services throughout the Southeastern United States. Further, Ms. Nettles serves on the Professional Development Council for the Atlanta Chapter of BOMA International.

BOMI also appreciates the efforts of its Education Division staff who participated in this book's production. They are: Michael J. Sallas, Vice President of Education; Mindy Gaines, Managing Editor; Alan Francis, Instructional Design Manager; Tara Mairs, Project Editor; Lori Pierelli, Project Editor; Lynn Jones, Book Designer; and Manny Sortillon, Special Projects Manager.

In addition, BOMI would like to acknowledge the following BOMI Staff members who assisted in the development of this book: Daniel B. Baum, President and members of the New Products Team: Jennifer Bundschu, Diane Mackey, Kristen McMullen, Darryl Pitt, and Randy Saba.

Preface

Successful performance as a property, facility, or systems maintenance manager requires vast knowledge, awareness, and mastery of a myriad of topics. Within the over 16,000 pages of information in BOMI's four professional designation programs, the RPA, FMA, SMA, and SMT, there are more than 30,000 topics. Truly, the building and facilities industry body of knowledge has evolved to the point that there is too much to be remembered. Yet, much of this information is critical to the health, safety, and commerce of the clients we serve as well as to local, state, and federal regulations. Today's building and facilities manager is accountable for all of this knowledge.

BOMI Institute's Reference Guides are designed to answer your everyday questions. The content includes bulleted lists, resources, processes, and procedures to strengthen on-the-job performance. In addition, each guide is arranged in an easy-to-use question and answer format. These Reference Guides are a help desk at your fingertips.

The mission of BOMI Institute is to provide learning opportunities that enhance individual performance and add value to organizations in the building and facilities industry.

The Practical Guide to Lease Development

BUILDING OWNERS AND MANAGERS INSTITUTE

Contents

Leasing Obligations, Covenants, and Clauses

Management and Building Owner Practices

Introduction

This Practical Guide explains the important components of a lease. The information presented will help property managers determine:

- what to look for in a lease
- the right questions to ask
- whom to ask when a lease is being negotiated and drafted

Although this guide is a valuable tool, it is not intended as a map to creating the perfect, lawsuit-resistant lease. Therefore, as a property manager, you must have a trusting relationship with a knowledgeable attorney. You will need a helpful ally to advise you about the many legal issues in the lease.

Commercial leases can be complicated. New terms, technological changes such as utility deregulation, and court decisions interpreting lease language can make it difficult even for experienced professionals to keep up. The document itself can be intimidating. Commercial leases can easily run from 10 to 50 or more pages when all the addenda, affidavits, guarantees, agreements, and exhibits are included.

Leasing Fundamentals

What are the first three steps in the lease drafting process?

1. **Define the lines of communication**: The lines of communication between attorney, property manager, and property owner need to be clearly established in the beginning of the lease development process. In addition, you must define responsibilities early on. If the property manager is to do all the negotiating, all parties must clearly understand this. Keep in mind that this is a team operation, yet someone has to be the captain; defining everyone's responsibilities at the beginning is important.

2. **Discuss preliminary issues**: After the lines of communication have been defined, discuss various preliminary issues such as improvements, rental rate, term, expense adjustments, and so forth. Once these preliminary issues have been settled, draft a letter of intent.

3. **Draft a letter of intent**: If both sides find the terms and conditions in these early negotiations acceptable, they will draft a letter of intent, or an offer to lease, covering the basic business terms. This document is signed by the prospective tenant and property owner.

What is a letter of intent?

The letter of intent, or an offer to lease, is the foundation for constructing the lease document. This letter covers many major issues, such as:

- length of lease
- rent
- additional rent
- options
- tenant improvement allowance
- other terms and conditions to which the parties have agreed

Sample Letter of Intent

September 8, 2004

Brookton Development Corp.
Attn: John Hall
Town Central Plaza
5560 Moosehead Drive, Suite 101
Bangor, ME 04401

RE: Old Town Shopping Mall

Dear Mr. Hall:

This letter confirms our intent to execute a lease (the "**Lease**") for one of the spaces (the "**Space**") in the Northwest Retail Lane at your Old Town Shopping Mall at the northwest corner of State Highway 2 and Baxter Drive in Bangor, Maine (the "**Shopping Center**"). Attached to this letter of intent is an initial deposit in the amount of $__________, which you may hold and apply to our obligations if and when we execute a definitive, written lease agreement.

Our intent to execute the Lease is subject to the following terms and conditions.

1. The Lease will be your standard form lease for spaces at Old Town Shopping Mall.

2. The gross rental square feet of the Space will be approximately __________ square feet. We prefer to occupy Space # __________; our second choice is Space #__________.

3. The minimum monthly basic rent for the Space shall be from Three and no/100 to Three and 50/100 Dollars ($3.00–$3.50) per square foot. Also commencing on the first day of November after the Lease begins, we will pay additional rent based upon changes in the Consumer Price Index ("**CPI**") since the commencement of the Lease, and the amount of this additional CPI rent will be adjusted each year on the same date.

4. We intend a triple net lease. We will be responsible for all taxes, utilities services, maintenance, repairs, insurance, etc. required in connection with the Space as well as our pro rata share of all other expenses of the Old Town Shopping Mall, including but not limited to common area maintenance expenses, taxes, insurance premiums, merchants association dues, etc. In addition, we will pay any privilege, excise, sales, gross proceeds rent, or other tax which arises in connection with the Lease.

5. The initial term of the Lease will be for a period of three (3) years. We will have the option to renew the Lease with not less than one hundred and eighty (180) days prior written notice for one (1) additional

three-year period upon the same general terms and conditions but at the then prevailing market rate of minimum basic rent as determined by you.

6. When we execute the Lease, we will pay you a security deposit equal to at least one month's minimum basic rent (our initial deposit above shall apply toward the total amount due) and we will prepay both the first and last month's minimum basic rent.

7. You will bear the cost of and be responsible for constructing and installing standard building shell improvements (the "**Shell Improvements**"); however, we will be obligated at our expense to construct and install all other improvements as well as our retail trade fixtures within the Space and will do so promptly so we can open for business within four (4) weeks after you complete the Shell Improvements. Except for the installation of our retail trade fixtures and inventory, we will use workers and contractors whom you employ or approve in writing to perform our work.

8. We will be entitled to use the Space for __________, subject, however, to reasonable use limitations which you establish to create an appropriate tenant mix within the Shopping Center, as set forth in the Lease.

9. The Shopping Center will have no less than the number of parking spaces required by local ordinance, and employee parking will be available.

10. The payment and performance of our obligations under the Lease will be guaranteed by our principals, members or shareholders upon your standard form guarantee.

This letter reflects our present understanding, however, the foregoing terms and conditions described are not intended to be all that will be contained in the Lease.

It is understood that neither you nor we will be bound or liable to the other by this letter until both of us execute a definitive written lease agreement.

We are looking forward to the opportunity to be a tenant at Old Town Shopping Mall.

Sincerely,

[COMPANY NAME]

By [NAME], [TITLE]

Address

Telephone

What is a lease?

A lease is a legal document that includes facts, obligations, and responsibilities of the owner (lessor) and tenant (lessee). This document is written in a language that is enforceable in court.

Leases are composed of elements (facts) and covenants (promises). Traditionally, covenants in a lease do not depend on each other. For example, a tenant might enforce lease terms that benefit the tenant even if the rent has not been paid. Similarly, if the landlord breaks its covenants to the tenant, the tenant is still liable for rent and must comply with all other duties to the landlord. Of course, a well-drafted lease should anticipate these problems by including language that makes the covenants dependent to avoid unfair or absurd results.

Although there are many different types of leases, nearly every type of commercial property lease addresses similar issues. A typical lease contains provisions describing the following elements and covenants:

- parties to the contract
- rent amount
- term and extension (if any)
- premises description
- tenant improvements
- assignment and subletting

- landlord's agreement to repair and/or improve
- lease provisions limiting liability
- methods for resolving disputes
- insurance coverage

The owner's covenants usually require the owner to:

- permit the tenant's use of the property
- make certain repairs
- furnish certain utilities (because of utility deregulation, the lease may also make the owner solely responsible for selecting the building's electric and telecommunications service providers)
- provide a variety of other services, such as maintenance

The tenant's covenants include:

- paying rent
- using the leased premises in a specified manner
- not subletting the space
- giving up the space in good condition at the end of the agreed term

The lease may also impose other conditions such as:

- paying taxes
- paying insurance
- paying utilities
- allocating liability for repairs

What is the purpose of a lease?

The purpose of a lease document is to try to define all of the obligations and responsibilities—in minute detail—between the owner and tenant. This is why commercial leases can be more than 100 pages long. Some of the meaning of these details may appear at first to be fairly straightforward. But after closer examination, more complex meanings emerge.

What do attorneys do in lease development?

While you, or the leasing agent, negotiated the basic business terms and conditions of the lease, in most cases an attorney prepares the lease document based on the information you provide. Depending on the size and complexity of the transaction, you may want to have an attorney help draft the letter of intent, or review it if the letter is provided by the tenant. No matter what the arrangement, the attorney represents the owner.

What laws apply to the lease document?

When interpreting a lease, the general rules of contract law apply. Such rules include:

- Any ambiguities in the document will be construed against the drafter of the document. This means that if any fact, covenant, or clause is not clear, any negative interpretation will be against the party who wrote the document.
- The lease document is intended as the entire agreement among the parties. Whatever you may have said or agreed to during negotiations is not enforceable if it isn't written down and included in the document.
- Words in the document should have a plain and ordinary meaning. In other words, the lease should not be written in ambiguous terms or a foreign language as a way to confuse one of the parties.

FYI

Be aware that, to avoid being penalized for ambiguous language, some attorneys try to circumvent general contract rules by including a catch-22 lease clause that states there is "no presumption against the drafter in the event of controversy." Judges may disregard this clause because it may be intended to trick somebody or used as an excuse not to be penalized for sloppy legal work.

What are the facts needed in a lease?

Leases need to contain a significant number of facts that must be presented in certain ways, including:

- **Name of parties**: The names of the landlord and tenant must be correct and properly spelled. Formal corporate names must be used, not "trading as" or "doing business as" names.
- **Signature blocks**: There must be signature lines for the landlord and each tenant. Signature blocks must be set up correctly with a signature date. After the lease is signed, make sure each signature has been dated.
- **Blanks**: All appropriate blanks must be filled in. "None" or "not applicable" can be inserted where necessary.
- **Deletions/amendments**: All parties must initial every deletion and amendment.
- **Attachments**: All the attachments that are referenced in the main body of the lease agreement must be attached. These documents must be clearly identified exactly as they are referenced. For example, if the body of the lease agreement refers to an "Addendum," the attachment should not be called an "Amendment." (Different types of attachments include addenda, amendments, exhibits, and riders.)

- **Accompanying documents**: Documents referenced in the lease, or required by the landlord, must be included with the lease. These documents can include a lease guaranty, the tenant's financial statement, or a lease summary sheet.
- **Lease date**: The lease must be dated. In addition, the rent commencement date and the length, or term, of the lease must be clearly defined.
- **Legal description**: The lease must contain a legal description of the property and a common name and/or address of the property.
- **Rental rate and other terms**: The lease agreement must clearly identify the rental rate and the basic terms of payment, escalations, CAM fees, expense stops, and all other monetary matters.
- **Special provisions**: Any special provisions or amendments must be included in the lease.
- **Federal, state, and local requirements**: The lease agreement must comply with all specific requirements of federal, state, and/or local laws, codes, and regulations, as well as any recently enacted or promulgated amendments. Your attorney may know about certain local lease laws to which the lease must conform. Depending on the situation, the lease may need language dealing

with OSHA (Occupational Safety and Health Administration) hazardous material disclosure or the ADA (Americans with Disabilities Act) compliance.

- **Social security number, federal ID number, and SIC (Standard Industrial Classification) Code**: These numbers must be in the lease to track personal or company dollars, as well as any environmental infractions.

What is the description of the premises?

The description of the premises explains the space the tenant is to occupy in detail. It should also state any additional space included in the lease, such as basement storage or rooftop telecommunications antenna locations. If additional space is included, the lease should explain the conditions of access for the tenant.

The lease should also state, usually in another clause, the parking rights (if any) for the tenant and its customers/visitors.

What is the commencement date?

The commencement date is the date the lease begins. This must be clearly stated to avoid confusion, such as whether the lease begins when the tenant starts alterations, or when the tenant commences business. Although it may be the same, the commencement date should not be confused with the date that lease payments begin.

FYI

One way to make sure everyone is clear about all the dates is to use an estoppel certificate. An estoppel certificate is an agreement between a tenant and landlord wherein the tenant certifies that the lease is in full force and effect; the date of commencement and expiration date are correct; the landlord has performed its part of the lease agreement to the date of the certificate; and there are no outstanding promises or agreements outside the lease.

Who are the parties to the lease?

There are two parties to a lease: the owner and the tenant. Sounds simple, right? What may sound simple contains deeper issues that carry far-reaching legal consequences. For example, unless the right questions are asked when naming the tenant in a lease, the lease may be faulty and unenforceable right from the beginning. The lease may name the wrong corporate entity or an entity that is not legally recognizable. Depending on the nature of the parties to the lease, different issues may arise. Entities that can be party to a lease include:

- corporations
- general partnerships
- limited partnerships
- limited liability companies and partnerships
- cotenants
- co-owners

What are corporations?

Corporations are legal entities organized under a state's business laws. A corporation can become obligated to fulfill its responsibilities under a lease by an officer of the corporation, such as the president, vice president, or a duly authorized executive. Accordingly, it is appropriate to ask for evidence of the necessary corporate approval before a lease is completed. Typically, either a board of directors will provide meeting minutes approving the transaction, or a resolution will specify the corporate officer who is authorized to sign on behalf of the corporation.

In addition to citing the proper name of the corporation in the lease, you may need to:

- Confirm the legal existence and good standing of the company.
- Check with the appropriate state government agency—usually the office of the secretary of state—to ensure that the corporation remains in good standing.
- Confirm compliance with all proper procedures. (For example, a corporation organized in one state but leasing property in another may have to complete a qualification or registration procedure as a foreign corporation.)

What are general partnerships?

General partnerships are partnerships wherein everyone shares the same responsibilities and liabilities. Unlike a limited partnership, a general partnership can be bound by any of its partners. When leasing to a general partnership, check the partnership agreement to make sure there is no restriction on the authority of a particular partner to bind the partnership.

What are limited partnerships?

Limited partnerships are legal entities wherein one of the many partners (called the general partner) assumes the responsibility for meeting obligations of the partnership. As with corporations, limited partnerships also must be in good standing in the state in which they are formed and may be subject to qualification or registration procedures in other states. Only a general partner may bind a limited partnership; therefore, limited partners should not sign the lease. When leasing to a limited partnership, check the partnership agreement that governs the structure of the limited partnership to determine whether the general partner is subject to any restriction regarding his or her authority to sign the lease.

What are limited liability companies and limited liability partnerships?

Limited liability companies and limited liability partnerships are business entities created by state statutes. These business entities combine the favorable tax benefits of a partnership with certain limited liability features of a corporation. Since the scope and authority of representatives of these business entities vary from state to state, check the relevant state statutes to ensure compliance when entering into a lease agreement.

What are cotenants?

Cotenants are two or more people or entities that lease the same space. When more than one person or entity is to be a tenant under a lease, make sure all tenants are named and each signs the lease.

What are co-owners?

Co-owners are two or more parties that own a property. (This may occur when there is family ownership.) All co-owners of the property must sign the lease as landlords. When a husband and wife own property as tenants by tenancy in entirety—the term used for co-ownership by a husband and wife—one spouse cannot bind the other spouse to a lease. Where ownership is by tenancy in common or joint tenancy—the terms used for types of co-ownership by two or more co-owners—one owner has no authority to bind his or her co-owners. States that recently enacted joint marital property laws may have additional requirements.

What is a lease guarantee?

A lease guarantee is a legal document often prepared by an attorney. It is a stand-alone document that may or may not be part of the lease. This document states that either an individual or some other entity (a guarantor) will pay the rent in the event the tenant doesn't. Many technical issues—ranging from how to serve legal notice to the tenant and guarantor to how long the guarantee will last—need to be detailed in the document. Before accepting a lease guarantee, always require the guarantor to provide financial statements and run a credit check.

FYI

In the lease, an owner may include a clause that explains if the guarantor dies or has diminished creditworthiness, the tenant may be in default on the lease because the guarantee is no longer viable.

What is a letter of credit?

A letter of credit is often a year-to-year commitment from a reputable financial institution confirming a financial obligation to the owner that the owner may draw upon if the tenant does not pay the rent. The tenant pays a fee, and/or interest, for the letter of credit. A lease clause about the letter of credit must detail how and when the owner may use it.

What is a security deposit?

A security deposit is usually one or two months of rent, which the tenant must give the owner at signing. The owner deposits this money into an escrow account and returns it to the tenant when the lease terminates—as long as all conditions of the lease have been met and there is no damage to the building. Several issues need to be clearly addressed in the lease regarding security deposits, including:

- Who gets the interest on the security deposit? (Ask your attorney if there are laws governing this.)
- Under what circumstances can the owner use the money in escrow?
- When and how is the security deposit returned to the tenant?

What is rent?

Rent is a payment by a tenant to the landlord to occupy the leased premises.

When and how is rent paid?

Rent is customarily paid on the first of the month; the lease should be very specific about when rent is due. Late payment usually incurs a late fee, the amount of which is explained in the lease.

Rent generally begins to accrue at the beginning of the lease term. Although, in leases where tenant improvements are being made to the leased premises, it is also common for the rent payments to begin upon possession by the tenant. A landlord may offer a period of free rent (called a rental abatement) to the tenant as an inducement, in which case some or all of the rental obligations are delayed until the free rent period has expired.

FYI

Be forewarned that if you continually accept late rent payments from a tenant, you might not be able to evict the tenant for chronic late payment. A judge could decide that because you consistently accepted late payments, you changed the due date of the rent, thus altering the terms of the lease.

Rent is paid in advance and does not become due until the applicable rental period begins. In an attempt to get around this, some landlords specify the entire aggregate amount of the rental obligation in the lease, then they add a provision that accelerates all future rents to make them immediately due and payable in the case of default. In some jurisdictions this clause is unenforceable. An accelerated rent clause may work when it ensures that the owner gets only what would be owed; it does not work as a tool to penalize the tenant.

What is fixed rent?

Fixed rent can mean both a monthly payment and rent without extras. When the tenant's only monetary obligation is the payment of a fixed rent, the lease may be called a gross lease. When the tenant pays not only a fixed rent but also other expenses—including operating costs, taxes, and insurance—the lease may be called a net lease, of which there are many variations.

What is rent escalation?

Rent escalation is a lease provision in which the landlord requires the tenant to pay a higher aggregate rent by adjusting the annual base rent by an agreed method during the term of the lease agreement. There are two reasons for this.

- to increase the building's revenue and, therefore, its value
- to ensure that the base rent will keep up with inflation

The most common way to escalate rent is through a procedure called stepped rent.

What is stepped rent?

Stepped rent is used when a tenant wants to lease the space but objects to the present asking rate. Stepped rent can be used in good markets as well as bad.

Assume that the asking rate is $20 per rentable square foot. By making the following adjustment, both the tenant and the landlord might be satisfied:

- Year one $18
- Year two $19
- Year three $20
- Year four $21
- Year five $22

The average rental rate over the five years is $20 per square foot. Although the landlord has a lower cash flow during years one and two, this loss is offset by higher rent values in years four and five, increasing the building's value.

In a strong market, of course, the owner can start out at $20 and increase each year by a fixed amount.

Stepped rent has many variations, depending on the need to make the deal and the creditworthiness of the tenant. If you are considering a stepped rent agreement, make sure the tenant has the capacity and integrity to pay the higher rent in the latter part of the lease.

How can the CPI (Consumer Price Index) be used to determine rent?

Every month the Bureau of Labor Statistics of the U.S. Department of Commerce publishes the CPI, which indicates changes in the cost of living. The CPI acts as a price indexing scale for the landlord to use in measuring the loss or gain of the dollar. By using this index to determine rent, the landlord can feel assured that the net rent is not eroding during the term of the lease.

A CPI clause in a lease should contain some of the following elements:

- identity of the particular index that is to be used since different indexes measure different items
- geographic coverage, such as the U.S. City Average or a local area index
- index base and base year
- percentage of the CPI increase that applies to and increases the base rent
- provision for a substitute replacement index if the particular CPI index is discontinued

In a soft market, and because of tenant experience with the economic situation during the early 1980s when the CPI rose dramatically because of rampant inflation, tenants may be reluctant to agree to this adjustment formula to the base rent.

The downside for the owner is that the building's expenses, or the overall CPI, may increase at a faster rate than the rate of the agreed upon escalation. It is a bonus for the owner, however, if the rent increases faster than expenses or the overall CPI.

What is a flat fixed-annual-percentage increase in base rent?

A flat fixed-annual-percentage increase in base rent is a way of escalating rent by increasing it by a fixed percentage each year. The disadvantage of a fixed-percentage increase is if the CPI goes higher than the fixed rate, the fixed rate will not be keeping up with inflation.

What is percentage rent?

Some leases for retail operations specify that rent is paid based on a percentage of the gross sales of the business against a base rent. While most office building leases are not based on percentage rents, you may have retail concession space you want to lease based on a percentage of the sales. This approach lets the owner participate in the success of the tenant. Some states restrict percentage rents, so if you decide to use this method, make sure it is legal in your state.

Profitable rents based on a percentage of sales require a tenant, such as a restaurant or store, that has experience operating a retail establishment. Good operators are also knowledgeable about what it takes to set up a retail establishment. They also may be sharp negotiators when it comes to owner contributions for tenant improvements and rent abatements.

A lease based on a percentage rent can be troublesome, because it is often difficult to learn the tenant's true gross sales. One way to solve this problem is to require the tenant to report his or her sales and then give your auditor permission to examine books and records. Make sure the lease lists all of the records the owner can examine. Your auditor should have access to:

- journals
- general ledgers
- all records that verify sales
- bank statements that verify income
- purchase invoices
- cash register tapes
- inventory records
- tax returns
- state and local sales tax reports

FYI

Most audit clauses specify that if the owner discovers an audit discrepancy exceeding what was reported, that amount, plus interest, is due the owner. If the discrepancy exceeds 5 percent, the cost of the audit will also be added to what the tenant owes the owner. If the amount exceeds 10 percent, the owner may have the option to cancel the lease.

What is base rent?

Base rent is the monthly recurring rental charges stated in the lease. Base rent may include an escalation formula. The purpose of this rent is to pay the owner's debt service, cover the depreciation expense, and provide a rate of return on the investment.

What is additional rent?

Additional rent is any and all charges besides base rent the tenant must pay according to the terms of the lease. Usually this means paying a portion of the expenses the owner incurs for operating the building. The exact mechanism for how this is done depends on how it is defined in the lease. There are many ways to calculate additional rent, so make sure the lease clearly outlines all charges.

FYI

The term *additional rent* may vary from area to area, and even from lease to lease. It might not even be used at all in your market because, depending on state tax laws, certain kinds of rent may not be taxable. The many tax implications of rent are a good reason to ask a real estate attorney who knows about taxes and commercial law to craft the lease.

The following is a list of items typically covered under additional rent. (Note that some of these items may also be classified as expenses.)

- ✦ building operating expenses
- ✦ annual expense adjustments
- ✦ CAM (common area maintenance) charges, such as those usually associated with retail malls
- ✦ late-payment fees for overdue rent
- ✦ legal fees and court costs to get the tenant to comply with the terms of the lease, or to enforce the owner's remedies
- ✦ collection costs for hiring a collection agency to obtain money owed from a current or former tenant
- ✦ expenses related to building repair
- ✦ miscellaneous fees, such as the bank charge in the event a tenant's check bounces

What are operating expenses?

The largest category of additional rent is usually operating expenses. A building's operating expenses are all of the costs incurred to manage and maintain the property. The tenant pays a portion of these expenses. Depending on the lease, tenants will pay one-twelfth of the annual operating expenses along with the base rent. Once a year—by a specific date stated in the lease—the owner prepares a statement of operating expenses to be paid by each tenant. This annual statement will reflect any increase or decrease in expenses.

There is no industry-wide standard definition of what constitutes operating expenses or CAM charges. Each lease must specify all eligible expenses, which could be 100-plus items in certain cases. If the definition of expenses in the lease is not complete, clear, and detailed, a tenant could successfully dispute some of the charges.

Operating expenses can add significant costs to the owner, so it is in the owner's interest to pass along as many expenses as possible. On the other hand, it is in the tenant's interest to limit the items that can be charged as an operating expense. Agreement on exactly what items will be charged to the tenant, along with how they are calculated, should be negotiated before the lease is signed.

What are CAM charges?

CAM charges are expenses incurred to maintain the sidewalks, parking lots, landscaping, and other common areas and common building systems. CAM charges are calculated for specific areas of the property (usually in retail malls). Typical common areas include:

- **Facilities provided for the common use or benefit of the tenants and/or public**: For example, corridors, lobbies, mechanical rooms, mail rooms, and restrooms
- **Vertical penetrations not for the exclusive use of any one tenant**: For example, elevators, stairwells, pipe shafts, and vents

FYI

It is common to manage a property with numerous leases, each lease containing discrete definitions of operating and CAM expenses. This is an accounting nightmare when it comes time to calculate the annual expense adjustment. Property management software that performs most of these calculations is often used. This software can also quickly identify leases that deviate from the building's "standard" expense categories when they are entered into the lease database. Expenses for leases with deviations may need to be manually calculated, an extremely difficult task. As a result, the accounting department customarily uses the expense definitions from the most liberal lease for calculating operating expense charges for the other tenants. This shortcut method may result in refunds in the event a tenant audits the lease.

What expenses cannot be charged to the tenant?

Items that cannot be charged to the tenant may include:

- capital improvements (except those that may reduce operating costs and thereby benefit all the tenants)
- debt service, depreciation, ground leases, and associated fees
- cost of altering other tenant spaces
- brokers' commissions
- marketing and legal costs associated with obtaining tenants
- excessive payments for goods and services affiliated with the owner
- services performed expressly for one tenant
- executive salaries and benefits above the property manager level
- costs of items that have already been reimbursed to the owner
- insurance or other sources
- late-payment charges or interest incurred when the owner fails to pay vendors or taxes in a timely manner

What is indemnification?

Indemnification assumes the tenant agrees to defend the owner against lawsuits over incidents occurring on the tenant's premises. For example, suppose a visitor of the tenant slips on the tenant's floor and is injured. The visitor sues the owner and the tenant. Since the owner is indemnified, the tenant pays the owner's legal fees and damages resulting from the lawsuit.

What is a waiver of subrogation?

A waiver of subrogation is an insurance company's ability to sue on behalf of, or in lieu of, the policyholder. When you see this in a lease, usually both the tenant and landlord have agreed to waive subrogation by their respective insurance companies. This means the insured's insurance company cannot sue the negligent party to recover money paid to the insured. For example, suppose the tenant's employee accidentally causes a fire that also damages the building. The owner's insurance company pays for repairs to the building. The tenant's insurance company pays for the tenant's loss of property. The owner's insurance company now tries to sue the tenant to recover what was paid out to the owner on building repairs. However, because both the tenant and the owner waived subrogation, the owner's insurance company (depending on complex state insurance laws) cannot sue the tenant.

Usually, the insurance companies of both the owner and the tenant must agree to the waiver of subrogation clause in the lease.

How are building rules handled in a lease?

Building rules are usually attached to the lease document as an exhibit, rider, or addendum. Certain rules must be set to keep the common areas and other spaces of the building under the owner's control, along with preventing tenants from interfering with one another. This requires specific rules governing a variety of activities inside the property. While many of these rules may seem tedious, they protect an owner from potential liability in a variety of situations and to ensure the owner's control over the building.

The owner must retain the flexibility to change the rules from time to time as necessary, and the tenant needs to be aware of this. Whenever changes are made, the tenant will want assurances that such changes will not increase costs or impose new costs. Both the owner and tenant should review building rules periodically to make sure they make sense.

How does the lease address the possible sale of the property?

Routinely, a clause in the lease states that once the building is sold, the owner is released from any further obligations to the tenant.

In a sale transaction, the buyer gets a deed to the property and an assignment of the leases from the seller to the buyer. In this way, there is usually a seamless transition in ownership as the new owner assumes the existing lease(s).

As a condition of sale, the buyer will want to confirm that the leases are valid and in force. The owner will need to get estoppel certificates from the tenants to confirm the conditions and terms of the leases.

How does the lease address utilities?

Since deregulation, many utilities compete for the owner's attention and business. The language of the lease must allow property managers to evaluate the efficiency, cost-effectiveness, and reliability of these different utility providers.

The choice of electricity and phone service providers—and who knows what else in the future—rests in the hands of the consumer. Your building houses two consumer groups: the owner and the tenants. Although this freedom of choice may now extend to both, depending on how utility laws are written, it may not be in the owner's interest to permit tenants to contract for their own utilities. Take electricity, for instance. Here are some of the many questions that can arise:

- How will the electric provider terminate service for a tenant who doesn't pay its bill?
- Are there potential property damage or safety issues affecting adjacent tenants in the event of a power cut-off?
- Will there be different kinds of wires, cables, and meter boxes scattered throughout the building?
- Who will control workers who come in to install and service equipment?

- Who pays for fire or building code fines stemming from improper installations?
- Could tenants demand that the owner switch to a cheaper provider for CAM areas as a way to cut expenses?

To prevent the building from turning into an overloaded socket of wires from cable, phone, electric, and other providers, the owner needs to retain control over provision of these services. (In some situations, the owner can even be the provider.)

The lease should have provisions:

- stating that the owner controls the selection of the providers
- requiring the tenant to cooperate in allowing access to the premises so providers can make repairs and installations
- releasing the owner from liability in the event of an interruption of service

FYI

As this area of law evolves, judges, regulatory agencies, and the market will proffer new interpretations on the requirements and responsibilities of all the parties-provider, owner, and tenant. Property managers will need to follow these developments closely.

How does the lease address technology?

Because of rapid changes in technology, leases must also be crafted to be flexible enough to include future technologies as yet unknown. For example, today, leases must take into account the phenomenal growth of the Internet and the marketing and revenue incentives for owners to create computer networks or to offer websites to tenants.

Tenants' communications antennas and satellite dishes need to be addressed in the lease. Leasing roof space for cell phone and other types of communications antennas is a relatively recent source of revenue for the owner. This sometimes includes space inside the building for related electrical equipment.

When agreeing to lease space for an antenna, try to avoid using the agreement the telecommunications company offers unless it can be modified so you can:

- ✦ keep control over the site
- ✦ ensure that there is no electrical or radio frequency interference for other tenants
- ✦ ensure that the equipment meets FCC (Federal Communications Commission) guidelines

- include language stating that the equipment does not create any type of a health hazard
- identify when equipment creating a hazard can be turned off

Small (roughly 40-inch) satellite dish antennas can create an issue if they are placed in the building's windows. Based on current FCC regulations, an owner may not interfere with the tenant's reception of video signals. This means the tenant may place a small dish antenna in a window, or other part of the building under its control, and the owner cannot object—as long as the antenna does not infringe on any common area of the building.

FYI

For more details about negotiating rooftop leases, see BOMA's (Building Owners and Managers Association's) *Telecommunications Guide: Model License Agreement Language and Lease Language*; and *Wired for Profit: The Property Management Professional's Guide to Capturing Opportunities in the Telecommunications Market.*

If the building is wired for a network that is running on a central server operated and maintained by either the owner or a vendor:

- The owner may need to add a clause to the lease detailing what type of physical and software backup arrangements are available if the system goes down.
- The clause should also spell out the degree of security the firewall provides against unauthorized computer hacking (penetration).
- There may also be a need for a confidentiality clause to clarify the privacy rights of all users.

As an owner or owner representative, you may want to limit responsibility for service interruption with similar wording used under the utility provider clauses.

What are some pitfalls of using a generic lease?

Use caution if you are trying to reduce legal fees by using a generic or master lease.

- Don't assume clauses in generic preprinted lease forms bought at office supply stores are legally valid in every jurisdiction.
- Once you have a signed lease that has been crafted by an experienced attorney, get that attorney's approval before using the lease as a model. (Some lawyers treat their leases as intellectual property and have lease documents copyrighted.)
- In some states you can keep a copy of a master lease in the word processor of your own computer, fill in the blanks, and give it to your attorney for review. In other states, however, you are not allowed to use fill-in-the-blank forms.
- Don't forget that each building you manage will require a lease that is adapted to that particular property. These changes may include revised clauses pertaining to additional rent, escalations, CAM charges, and so forth.

Lease Obligations, Covenants, and Clauses

What are the owner's basic obligations?

The owner's basic obligations to the tenant are:

- covenant of quiet enjoyment
- covenant of possession
- warranty of fitness

What are some owner obligations to the tenant?

Owners also have certain duties to tenants. These include the duty to:

- disclose dangerous conditions
- inspect and repair public use premises
- maintain common areas under the owner's control

What is the covenant of quiet enjoyment?

The covenant of quiet enjoyment assures tenants that they will have peaceful possession of the property, free of interference from the acts or claims of the owner or certain third parties claiming rights through the owner. The tenants are protected from title disputes between the owner and anyone claiming superior title. Generally, even without a specific covenant, quiet enjoyment is implied in any owner/tenant relationship. Condemnation of the leased premises is generally not a violation of the owner's covenant of quiet enjoyment. Furthermore, a covenant of quiet enjoyment does not require the owner to repair leased premises.

What is the covenant of possession?

Provided the tenant is not in default, the covenant of possession gives the tenant exclusive possession and control of the premises. An owner cannot enter the tenant's property unless the owner reserves specific entry rights in the lease. Ordinarily, the lease states that the owner can come onto the property to accomplish owner obligations, such as to complete any required repairs, without disturbing the tenant's business. In addition, the owner may specify the right to enter the premises near the end of the term to show the premises to potential tenants. Without these kinds of specifically drafted exceptions, the landlord usually has no right to enter the premises, make repairs, or curtail a nuisance.

What is constructive eviction?

Constructive eviction enables the tenant to break the lease if the owner interferes so much with the tenant's use of the premises—such as failing to provide utilities—that the tenant is forced to leave.

What is the warranty of fitness?

A warranty of fitness ensures that the leased premises are suitable for the purposes anticipated by the tenant. If this warranty is included in the lease by the owner, then its application becomes a matter of contract interpretation. Unlike a warranty of habitability, which may be implied in residential leases, a majority of jurisdictions have found that there is no implied warranty of fitness in leases of property for commercial purposes.

What are the tenant's obligations?

The tenant has duties and liabilities including:

- paying rent
- not disturbing other tenants
- maintaining leased property

What are the tenant's rent-paying obligations?

One of the hallmarks of an owner/tenant relationship is the obligation of the tenant to pay rent by a certain time of the month. Rent is distinguished from other amounts that the tenant may have to pay to the owner, such as:

- security deposits
- late fees
- penalties
- CAM (common area maintenance) charges
- the tenant's share of utilities

Leases should generally anticipate changes and circumstances that may affect rent payment. Well-drafted leases contain provisions ending, or abating, rent in case of partial or complete destruction of the leased premises, for example. Many leases (at least in the commercial context) also contain provisions that accelerate future rent obligations if a tenant defaults.

Many multi-year leases also include provisions that increase rent according to inflation. (For example, some rent rates are tied to the CPI [Consumer Price Index].) In addition, many shopping center commercial leases have percentage rent. (That is, rent is paid to the shopping center landlord based on the gross sales volume of the tenant.)

CPI (Consumer Price Index)

An index used to measure cost of living increases that is calculated by the U.S. Department of Labor's Bureau of Labor Statistics.

FYI

Rent obligations differ from loan obligations. Unlike a loan, the obligation to pay rent does not become a liability on the tenant's books until after it is past due. For instance, if rent is paid monthly, the lease creates no debt until it is time for the monthly rental payment. Another feature distinguishing rent from a loan repayment is that loan payments are paid after debt is accumulated; rent is paid in advance.

What does the tenant obligation not to disturb other tenants mean?

Not disturbing other tenants means a tenant's business should not cause any problems for neighbors, such as:

- noise caused by employees or business processes
- clutter in common areas and hallways
- solicitation of business
- violation of building rules
- violation of local ordinances
- general nuisances

How must a tenant care for and repair a leased property?

A tenant's care and repair duties depend on the terms negotiated in the lease and on the nature of the leased property. Under a long-term lease for an entire building, the duty to repair usually falls to the tenant because the tenant is in the best position to do the repairs. On the other hand, in a multi-tenant building, a landlord is usually obligated to make repairs to the common areas, roof, and building exterior.

What is a lease clause?

Leases are composed of sections of words called clauses, which cover specific subjects. Some clauses in a lease are boilerplate, or standard.

Some examples of these standard boilerplate clauses include:

- indemnification
- severability
- governing law
- attorney's fees
- entire agreement
- condemnation
- eminent domain
- destruction

FYI

Always be sure to read all of the clauses of a lease—even if they are boilerplate—and ask an attorney to explain what you don't understand. If anybody tells you "don't worry, it's just boilerplate," read it twice. Poorly worded boilerplate clauses could be significant later if there is a tenant dispute that goes to court.

What is a lease audit clause?

A lease audit clause specifies how and when a tenant may conduct an audit of lease elements such as operating expenses and CAM charges. The following are some issues a lease audit clause should address:

- ✦ Specify the number of days after receiving the annual statement within which the tenant must give reasonable, written notice to the owner of intent to examine books and records.
- ✦ Specify the number of times a tenant can perform an audit. Owners can prevent the same tenant from auditing every year by permitting audits only every two years.
- ✦ If the tenant finds a discrepancy and wants to challenge the expenses, a notice stating this fact must be given to the landlord within a specific number of days. (Again, the procedures for this process should be detailed in the lease.)
- ✦ No matter what the issue is, the lease should state that the tenant is still liable for paying the rent and expenses while the dispute over expenses is being resolved.
- ✦ The audit clause should also state how and when your records will be accessible and a procedure for making your staff available to answer questions.

- If the audit turns up significant differences, try to settle and avoid going to court. No owner wants to be known as a cheater. Include wording in the lease—such as an arbitration clause—to open the way for negotiations and a settlement.
- Require a nondisclosure clause to prevent the tenant's auditing firm from using the results for marketing purposes.

When it comes to operating expenses and CAM charges, courts in some jurisdictions have found that tenants have an implied right to audit the owner's books with respect to operating expenses. Savvy tenants require an audit clause during negotiations and will later hire an outside firm that specializes in lease audits to check expense charges. To regulate the scope of this right to audit, the clause needs to specify the details governing an audit. Include a limitation on how far back in time a tenant's audit can reach; this should be the same as the statute of limitations (about four years, unless fraud is proven).

Deal in a straightforward manner with tenants when it comes to their audit rights. The owner who recognizes the tenant's right to audit has a powerful retention tool at lease renewal time. Tenants want to know what they are being billed for, so you must keep accurate records.

What is an expense stop?

An expense stop is a limit to the maximum amount of expenses the owner will pay. The amount of the expense stop is often the expenses incurred in the first (base) year of the lease. Consequently, in future years of the lease, the tenant is responsible for expenses that are greater than those incurred in the first year of the lease. This prevents rising expenses from eating into the owner's income.

What is an expense cap?

An expense cap sets a maximum amount of expenses a tenant will pay. For example, a tenant may agree to pay a prorated share of the property's expenses that exceed the base year expense stop, but will insist on limiting risk by capping the increase at a reasonable amount.

What are insurance clauses?

Insurance clauses are lease provisions that cover fire, liability, casualty, and other damage and liability issues. These clauses can be confusing. In fact, lease negotiations can even get bogged down because of them.

One way to avoid making a mistake is to have the building's insurance broker look at any insurance-related clauses in the lease. If you have any questions or concerns, ask the broker to check the pages that might influence the insurance clause. You may even want to ask the broker for a written analysis of the insurance clauses including any suggestions to ensure that the ownership is adequately protected.

Insurance is not a subject to learn about after a loss. Don't hesitate to call your broker with any questions you may have. Make a point to read the insurance policies covering your building. A property manager should never start reading the policies for the first time as the firefighters are leaving the building.

What are some common insurance requirements?

Insurance coverage types and amounts may be mandated by insurance carriers or by law. Most leases require the following:

- ✦ The owner must have fire, extended perils, and liability insurance on the building.
- ✦ The owner should obtain workers' compensation and liability insurance on its employees.
- ✦ The tenant must keep fire and liability insurance on personal property and tenant improvements.
- ✦ The tenant should obtain workers' compensation and liability insurance on its employees.
- ✦ The tenant must provide certificates of insurance to the owner to show proof of coverage.
- ✦ The owner should be named "additional insured" in tenants' policies.

FYI

Without proof of coverage, a victim of an accident on a tenant's premises can sue both the tenant and owner. If the owner isn't named "additional insured" in the tenant's policies, the tenant's insurance company has no obligation to defend the owner. The owner's insurance company will then have to defend the owner.

Make sure the lease requires the tenant to use a financially sound insurance company licensed to do business in your state. From time to time, insurance companies go out of business and policyholders learn there is no money to cover a loss. To avoid having a tenant use a low-premium but financially shaky insurer, insist that the company be rated good to excellent on its claims-paying ability by raters such as Standard and Poor's or A. M. Best. All insurance brokers should be able to provide this rating information.

What are some typical occupancy clause issues?

The lease should also contain clauses that specify certain conditions governing the occupancy of the building. These conditions range from agreements on how a tenant may expand space to rules such as when the freight elevator can be used.

What is the expansion clause, or option?

The expansion clause details how the owner can make more space available to the tenant. If the tenant's business is expanding, chances are it may need more room. This possibility is addressed in the expansion clause. Usually these terms are agreed upon and are made part of the lease during negotiations.

The expansion clause must detail:

- where the expansion space is located
- the rent of the expansion space
- the procedure to exercise the expansion option (including the number of days the tenant has to give notice to the owner that it wants to lease the space)
- how any tenant improvements or owner improvements will be made

In the event the owner cannot allocate more space to meet the tenant's needs, the tenant may want to terminate the lease and seek space in another building. In general, the lease contains language that permits the tenant to move out if the owner cannot provide the space and as long as the tenant meets certain lease termination conditions.

What are the mechanisms for expansion?

Various mechanisms enable a tenant to expand within the building, usually into adjacent space. Whichever mechanism you use, make sure to avoid the mistake of giving the same option to more than one tenant, or you may have two or more tenants claiming the space at the same time.

The mechanisms for expansion are:

- **Expansion clause, or option**: This gives the tenant the right to expand.
- **Right of first refusal**: In the event that space is available, and the owner has an acceptable offer on it from a third party, the owner must first give the tenant the opportunity to match the offer.
- **Right to first option**: Occurs when the owner commits to delivering—and the tenant agrees to take—a negotiated amount of space at some point in the future.

FYI

The right to first option works best when the owner knows that the lease of another tenant in adjacent space will be expiring at a time when the tenant with the right to first option will want the space. The drawback is that if the space is vacant, the owner may need to find a short-term tenant until the other tenant exercises its rights.

What are condemnation and reconstruction clauses?

Condemnation and reconstruction clauses outline tenant and owner obligations if a government agency condemns all or part of the property or a catastrophic event, such as a fire, damages the building and prevents the tenant from occupying the leased space.

In either event, the condemnation and reconstruction clauses must contain specific language detailing:

- when rent obligations will cease
- criteria for determining the extent of damage
- owner's responsibilities for repair
- method of notification and deadlines
- limitations of repair or reconstruction
- how the tenant can prove he or she can repair the damage to the leased space before obligating the owner to repair the entire building
- the circumstances under which the owner can terminate the lease in the event of damage to the building

If a government agency condemns the property, the condemnation clause may need to state that the lease will automatically terminate a day before the condemnation is effective, to prevent the tenant from sharing in the condemnation payment.

A lease without such language could allow the tenant legal rights to claim part of the condemnation payment because of the loss of the value of any renewal options in the lease.

If the building is damaged by fire, a tenant could force the owner to rebuild even if it is not in the owner's interest to do so. In some cases, the owner may also end up paying out of pocket for tenant improvements not covered by insurance.

To avoid these situations, have your insurance broker and attorney read these clauses, along with any proposed changes that the tenant asks for during negotiations. Changes that seem insignificant could have big consequences. For example: The tenant seeks to have the phrase "insurable perils replace insured perils" in the damage clause. This language alters the definition of the owner's liability from repair from perils specifically covered by the insurance policy to a blanket statement meaning all perils that could be insured against. Specifically, if something occurs that is not covered by the owner's insurance, the owner is still responsible for repair.

What is an early termination, or downsizing, clause?

An early termination, or downsizing, clause enables the tenant to end the lease and move out. From an owner's perspective, a termination clause may not be much of an issue as long as there is a way to compensate the owner for an early termination. Conditions and deadlines about how to exercise such a clause also must be specified.

What is a relocation clause?

The relocation clause benefits the owner by giving the flexibility to rearrange the building's floor plan by moving a smaller tenant to another location in the building. You can expect this clause to be heavily negotiated. The owner usually offers to pay the tenant for any improvements and moving costs, as well as other agreed-upon costs.

What are assignment and subletting clauses?

An assignment clause transfers all the rights in the lease and leased premises to a third party.

A subletting (also known as subleasing) clause transfers a limited interest in the total space leased to a third party for the entire term of the lease.

A lease gives a tenant a certain legal interest in the space being rented. It is not in the owner's interest to relinquish total control of the space, so you should keep specific rights regarding assignment and subletting.

Unless the owner maintains some control over the tenant's right to assign or sublet, the owner may be unpleasantly surprised to find different, and less creditworthy, occupants in the space. Even worse is finding out that the new occupant is paying a higher rent to the original tenant, who continues to pay the owner the rent agreed upon in the lease. Another problem for the owner is losing control of the tenant mix by not having any say in who may occupy the leased space.

The way to control these types of problems is for the lease to define rights regarding assignment and subletting. The owner generally reserves the right to deny the tenant the ability to assign or sublet the lease, based on reasonable grounds.

To further protect the owner, the subletting and assignment clauses should include wording that requires the tenant to notify the owner or property manager in the event of a change in ownership of the tenant's corporation of 50 percent or more. This ensures that the owner knows who the tenant's ownership structure is if the tenant sells the company to another party, merges, or is acquired by either a related or unrelated corporate entity.

Some tenants will want the right to assign and sublet the lease to an affiliate without the written consent of the owner. This may be negotiable, as long as the owner has a way to guarantee that the original tenant remains responsible for meeting the terms of the lease.

FYI

In retail leasing try never to allow assignment or subletting unless the new occupant of the space will use it for the same purpose as the departing occupant (a Friendly's for a Ruby Tuesday's, a Lane Bryant for a Casual Corner, and so on). Subleases have been successfully blocked by owners because the new tenant's business was different from that which was stated in the language of the original lease.

What are subordination and nondisturbance clauses?

A subordination clause defines the lease as subordinate to another legal interest or claim. The owner requires the subordination clause to finance or sell the building without interference from the tenant. Many tenants request a nondisturbance clause in exchange for agreeing to a subordination clause.

A nondisturbance clause protects the tenant's rights granted by the lease from third party interference.

Owners routinely pledge their properties to a financial institution as collateral for a mortgage loan. Often, this is when subordination and nondisturbance clauses come into play. The tenant needs the nondisturbance clause so that the lease will not be terminated or modified after a refinancing or sale of the building.

These clauses become an issue if the owner fails to make mortgage payments and the mortgage holder forecloses on the property. The mortgage holder could interfere with a tenant's lease, such as evicting the tenant from the building, depending on the effective dates of the lease and mortgage. The interest of the mortgage holder (lender) in the owner's property is superior to the tenant's interest if the mortgage was entered into prior to the lease. In this case, the mortgage holder can terminate the tenant's lease upon foreclosure of the mortgage.

A tenant with a lease signed before the mortgage was made usually has more protection from eviction in the event the lender forecloses on the property, provided there is no subordination clause in the lease.

A tenant with a lease signed after the mortgage was made has no protection from eviction in the event of foreclosure, unless the lender has signed a nondisturbance agreement.

What is a recordation clause?

Depending on the law in your area, a tenant can have its lease recorded just as you would a title on a property. A recordation clause can keep the tenant from doing this.

An owner may want to prevent recordation because:

- ✦ If a tenant goes out of business or bankrupt, it can be time consuming and costly to get the recorded document removed.
- ✦ It could override the subordination clause by putting the lease in a better position than subsequent mortgages. (An owner seeking future financing may have a problem after the lender orders a title search and learns a tenant has recorded a lease that contains, say, a purchase option.)
- ✦ The lease becomes public record. Anyone can then learn all the terms and conditions of what, up to that point, had been a private business transaction. (This may be avoided by recording a "memorandum of lease," which summarizes some lease terms without disclosing rental rates and other sensitive information.)

Tenants may want to record the lease to protect their rights in the lease, such as an option to purchase.

What is an estoppel clause?

An estoppel clause in the lease usually relates to the owner's refinancing or sale of the building. The estoppel clause requires the tenant to complete a document called an estoppel certificate, which says to a third party (such as a lender or buyer) that the lease is in full force and there are not any defaults.

This estoppel certificate usually:

- states the date the lease commenced
- confirms that all work the owner promised to do has been done
- lists any changes to the lease
- states if there are any issues that might affect the payment of rent

Another feature of the estoppel certificate is that once the tenant gives it to the owner, the tenant is prevented from making any legal claims against the owner based on matters covered by the certificate, unless the basis for such claims is stated in the certificate.

FYI

The lease should provide a thorough explanation of what the certificate should say, who drafts it, and deadlines for when the owner demands it. Attaching a form of the certificate to the lease is advisable. If the tenant fails to provide the certificate, he or she can technically be held in default. Another option is to have the lease state that if the tenant fails to provide the certificate within the deadlines given by the owner, then "tenant shall be deemed to have agreed with the matters set forth therein," which becomes an estoppel certificate by default. Whether this estoppel certificate by default will be accepted by a third party, or a judge, is questionable.

Management and Building Owner Practices

What can I do to avoid problems during the leasing process?

If you sense trouble, here are some rules to follow that might help you avoid problems:

- **Keep your attorney in the loop**: When the tenant's attorneys want to have certain lease clauses modified, they should be directed to you, and you should pass these requests along to your attorney to determine whether they are acceptable.
- **Be sensitive to conflict**: If necessary, act as the intermediary between the two attorneys so that any issue that could affect the outcome of the transaction does not get bogged down and end up in a deadlock. (Often it is better to let an attorney negotiate directly with the tenant's attorney over legal terms as long as there is the understanding that no decisions can be made without the approval of the ownership.)
- **Review all legal documents before they go out**: Mistakes can range from simple typos or inserting the wrong name of the tenant, to an incorrect legal description of the property or poorly worded complicated insurance clauses. You do not need to understand every legal term, but you should try to check all documents' facts for accuracy.

A good real estate attorney is a critical link in the leasing team and can help promote a successful leasing process. The attorney can anticipate legal and business problems and provide solutions that protect the owner's interests. Yet, unfortunately, there are too many stories about attorneys who, in their zeal to represent their client, have killed a deal by nitpicking the details, involving themselves too deeply in the negotiations, or offering their opinions as to whether the deal is a good business transaction.

FYI

An alternative to reviewing all legal documents yourself is to hire a proofreader on an hourly basis to read the documents. In many cases, you will work from a standard form lease that has been reviewed and approved by the owner and the owner's attorney. In these situations you need to only review deviations from the standard form.

How can I create a user-friendly lease?

Leases are usually long documents, but despite their size, they follow a logical sequence. You can ask your attorney to include some simple things in a lease to make it easier to understand. Here are some suggestions for creating a user-friendly lease:

- Because of the length of commercial leases, and the many clauses, addenda, and other attachments, include a table of contents that lists all clauses and exhibits so they can be found easily during later discussions.
- A clause at the beginning of the lease defining the key terms (base rent, common areas, service areas, business hours) can help eliminate ambiguity.
- Instruct your attorney to use standard $8\frac{1}{2} \times 11$ paper, not 11×14 legal paper, (which is being phased out in the legal system) unless its use is stipulated in your legal jurisdiction or for other reasons. Standard paper does not require changing paper trays in printers and copiers and can be filed easily in standard-size cabinets.
- Leases also can be written in the language of formal law or in plain English. Always ask to have any legal document written so that you and your tenant can understand it on the first reading.

- Leases are constantly evolving; they always contain new and different clauses. As a property manager, you should keep up with clauses that could affect the operation of your building.

FYI

One way to keep up with leasing issues is to subscribe to various trade magazines and other publications that feature articles on leasing issues. Examples are *Building Operating Management, Real Estate Forum, Buildings, Commercial Property News,* and *The Wall Street Journal.* In addition, certain monthly newsletters devote their pages to changes and trends in real estate law. One comprehensive source on commercial real estate clauses is Brownstone Publisher's *The Insider's Best Commercial Lease Clauses.* This is an excellent reference work derived from their monthly newsletter *Commercial Lease Law Insider.* Another widely used source is Warren Gorham & Lamont, a firm that publishes real estate resources. Also, whenever possible, attend seminars sponsored by BOMA, IREM (Institute of Real Estate Management), and other real estate organizations.

How do I make sure the rent gets paid?

To make sure rent is paid, include clauses in the lease that guarantee the lease and/or a security deposit. Each works differently and may be governed by complex law.

How do I control legal fees?

To help keep legal bills from ballooning out of control:

- Don't distract attorneys with unnecessary calls or demands on their time; keep discussions short and to the point.
- Keep attorneys focused on the assignment, and don't let them stray into areas like negotiations, unless that is part of their job.
- Provide attorneys with all the facts and details they need to do their job. You will be charged when they do the homework you should have provided, such as obtaining certain corporate documents, financial statements, and copies of legal documents filed with government agencies or those that may need notarizations or certification from the tenant.

- Avoid last-minute rush jobs; if a deadline is important, the property manager needs to make this clear to the attorneys so they can prioritize their time.

Attorneys often bill by the hour or by a negotiated flat fee. Your agreement with an attorney should be put into writing, and many attorneys will have you sign a retainer agreement. The agreement should indicate if there is a lower rate structure when paralegals are used to perform certain parts of the work. If any aspects of the billing practices are unclear, do not hesitate to ask for clarification.

How do I calculate operating expenses and CAM charges?

Several formulas can be used to determine the percentage of expenses a tenant will pay. For example:

- ✦ Divide the rentable area of the tenant's space by the rentable area of the property, excluding parking facilities. This method spreads out the expenses over all the rentable space in the building, rented or not, and creates a lower percentage and fewer expenses, which favors the tenant.
- ✦ Divide the rentable area of the tenant's space by the rented area of the property. This creates a higher percentage and greater expenses charged to the tenant, therefore favoring the owner.
- ✦ Divide the rentable occupied space by the rented area of the property. This method further diminishes the area for which expenses can be allocated, causing an even larger increase in the percentage charged to the tenant.

The definition of the size of the tenant's space also varies. Is it, for example, the square footage of the entire office suite? Or is it the usable area, in which case the space allotted for columns, partitions, and closets is deducted? This definition must be agreed upon by all parties and clearly stated in the lease.

Both the agreement on charges and how they are calculated should be negotiated before the lease is signed. Once an agreement is reached, add the specifics to the lease.

How should I handle the building temperature and tenant complaints?

It is not always in the owner's interest to be too exact about certain lease obligations. A good example is the building's interior temperature. A statement about heating and cooling usually lies somewhere in the building's rules. You can't make every tenant happy with heating and air conditioning. No matter what you do, someone may be too hot or too cold.

If the building's HVAC systems are unable to perform to standards set in the lease, the tenant might claim a default under the lease and sue the owner for damages and/or loss of present and future business for failure to perform. Further, the tenant might file an enforcement action requiring the owner, at the owner's expense, to make all modifications to the equipment necessary to satisfy the tenant's temperature requirements.

To reduce complaints:

- Don't specify temperatures for the space by degrees or performance ratings of the building's HVAC system in the lease or building rules.

- If you have to specify temperatures, give yourself some room with qualifying language such as "under the reasonable control of the landlord;" even the most sophisticated HVAC equipment will have difficulty adjusting to radical outside temperature changes.
- Make sure the building rules contain language requiring the tenant to help reduce the problem (for example by closing blinds on the sunny side of the building) before complaining about inadequate air conditioning.

How can I make sure tenants are following the building's rules?

It makes no sense to bully a tenant about the provisions of the lease if the principal goal is to keep the occupancy of the building as high as possible—especially if available space far exceeds demand. Both parties should keep and enforce lease covenants, but enforce the provisions within the scope of reality and common sense.

Take, for example, the tenant who is having difficulty paying rent. The property manager should think about easing the circumstances rather than forcing an eviction suit, even though the tenant may have violated the provisions of the lease. This can be accomplished by either reducing or abating the rent for a period of time to give the tenant an opportunity to recover. While this may seem counterintuitive, consider the cost of replacing the tenant.

How do I keep track of all of the leases in a multi-tenant building?

Keep track of multiple tenants by keeping a lease summary covering the key details of each lease. This is fairly easy if the building you are managing has five tenants. It becomes an extraordinary task when the building has hundreds of tenants, like the Sears Tower in Chicago.

One solution is to computerize all real estate files. Many companies sell real estate management software that integrates financial statements, bookkeeping functions, and tenant information. Some examples include:

- CTI (Comprehensive Technologies International, Inc.) Real Estate System
- RealWare
- Yardi
- Intuit, Inc. Real Estate Solutions

This software enables you to generate customized reports, such as a lease summary that can be sorted by name and date of expiration, size of space, or any other criteria. A list sorted by expiration date, for example, allows the property manager plenty of advance notice to create a renewal strategy.

To be useful, a lease summary, or lease abstract, needs to contain at least the following information:

- ✦ name of the tenant
- ✦ contact person and party to serve legal notice
- ✦ location (postal address, name of building, room or suite number)
- ✦ square footage of leased space
- ✦ rent escalations
- ✦ operating expense/CAM (common area maintenance) escalations
- ✦ expense exclusions/adjustments
- ✦ lease term
- ✦ expiration date
- ✦ notations if there are significant modifications to the master lease
- ✦ renewal, expansion, and cancellation options
- ✦ security deposit
- ✦ termination options

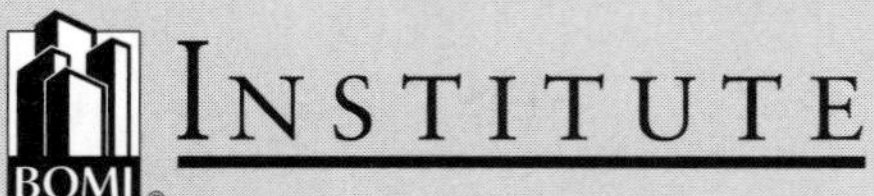

The Practical Guide to Lease Negotiations

Lease Negotiations

BUILDING OWNERS AND MANAGERS INSTITUTE

Contents

Lease Negotiation Strategies and Tactics

Leasing Retail Space

Introduction

Leasing property is a difficult type of real estate sale. A marketing plan helps you identify and target prospective tenants. But how do you find tenants and sell to them? You may doubt that you can be a successful salesperson. Sales work can have a high rate of rejection, but try not to take it personally. As they say, it's just business.

Sales is hard work, so to be successful, you need to know your building and the market conditions. In addition, you must be able to convey the correct message to the right prospective tenant at the right time.

Finding the prospective tenant requires some homework and legwork. Although effort alone will not guarantee results—it is not only how hard you work, it is also how smart you work. This guide covers the various ways of prospecting for tenants.

This guide also presents several sales basics. To learn more, spend some time with an experienced, successful broker and learn as many techniques as he or she is willing to share. You may also consider attending sales training courses taught in seminars or through local schools.

Lease Negotiation Fundamentals

What is negotiation?

Negotiation is the process of bringing two sides to an agreement about terms and conditions. This begins the moment you respond to a question about the space from a prospective tenant.

Knowing the business goals your building must meet to reach the owner's financial objectives is academic; negotiating and achieving them is an art form.

When negotiating:

- ✦ Try to keep things simple and friendly.
- ✦ Do not let poor attitude, ignorance of leasing procedures, or greed interfere with negotiations.
- ✦ Have patience when the process gets bogged down.
- ✦ Maintain your professionalism and do not let yourself get frustrated.
- ✦ Allow leasing agents to earn commissions and to fill that vacant space.
- ✦ Do not let any obstacles become personal or cloud your judgment.
- ✦ If you feel there is a problem, such as a stalled deal, approach the building owner first for guidance. In addition, call your prospective tenant, explain the situation, and seek a resolution that may salvage the deal.

What personal skills are needed for successful negotiations?

In the early stages of negotiations it is important to establish yourself as a straight shooter, rather than someone who wastes time playing games. You can help yourself establish a reputation for credibility and reliability by:

- knowing your product and sticking to the facts, not embellishing or misrepresenting them
- being careful about saying too much too soon and thus tipping your hand
- avoiding saying negative things about competing buildings or their management

By the time you begin to put proposed terms and conditions down on paper, as in a letter of intent or a proposal, you should have developed a feel for the prospect that allows you to create a more specific negotiating strategy.

What are four keys to successful negotiating?

Know how to listen: Listening is an art. After each conversation you have with the prospect, write down what you heard, and think about every point that the prospect made. Keep your notes so you can refer to them before follow-up meetings.

Know when to stop talking: The time for you to talk is when you are presenting the building and all the benefits of tenancy to the prospect for the first time. Learning when to stop talking and to start listening to the prospect is important. The time to listen and not interrupt is when the prospect tells you the features of the building that he or she likes, as well as the motivation for moving. Focus on these bits of information as you negotiate a lease.

Know what is really important: Never lose a deal over a couple of gallons of paint. You cannot always assume that the business terms of a proposed lease are going to be the most important issues. Factors such as the color of the wall covering, the texture of the carpet, accent lighting in the reception area, and soundproofing in the conference room, though merely aesthetic, may be important to the prospect. Even though these issues might be the furthest things from your mind as you concentrate on the major terms and conditions, be sensitive and listen. The flexibility to meet the prospect's needs and wishes on these types of details might gain you an edge.

Know how much authority you have: While you need someone in authority to guide you and approve decisions, direct owner involvement in the leasing or negotiating process is not usually helpful unless the owner has sharp sales skills. In general, the best way an owner can enhance the success of the leasing campaign is to stay in the background and allow you to act as the agent who engineers the deal. On occasion, however, the prospect will insist on involving the owner, and you may have to take that risk to secure the lease.

Both you and your prospect will be trying to achieve certain terms and conditions. Nothing is wrong with seeking an advantage over the other. After all, this is business.

How do I find tenants?

Tenants are most commonly found through:

- brokerage companies
- tenant referrals
- walk-ins
- phone inquiries
- networking
- canvassing
- cold-calling

What are brokerage companies?

A brokerage company is a third party that interacts between a buyer and a seller to complete a purchase agreement. There are numerous brokerage companies in the real estate industry who connect prospective tenants with owners who have space to lease. If you decide to use a brokerage company, be sure to check the company's reputation within the industry and compare fees with other providers.

What are tenant referrals?

Prospecting for tenants can begin with your current tenants. Make sure to get the word out and be creative about it. The most common ways to do this are:

- speaking with each of the decision makers in your building
- sending out letters to the decision makers, as well as the executives of each firm
- asking for referrals, possibly as a postscript, in any general letters to tenants (boxing it as an ad in the building newsletter, for example)

FYI

You can offer a bounty, such as a one-time reduction in rent, or a gift, to anyone who refers a lead for a new tenant that turns into a successful lease. Make sure you do not word the offer so that it becomes a commission because this could conflict with broker licensing laws as well as become a problem if an agent presents a referral.

What are walk-ins?

Walk-ins are people who show up at your office and want to know about leasing space in the building. This is one of the best and easiest ways to lease space because the prospect comes to you. Yet working with a walk-in is a lot like fishing: it is not hooking the fish that is hard; it is getting the fish into the boat without having it fall off the hook. Try not to let the walk-ins walk out.

A walk-in can happen at any time, so you and your office staff must be prepared in the following ways:

- If space is available, it should be in good condition and ready for showing. This means you need to remove the previous tenant's leftovers, repair any damage, and paint the space, if necessary.
- The building's common areas should be clean and presentable.
- Have plans ready. This includes floor plans for the entire building (usually reduced in size) that graphically show the location of the vacant space and as-built drawings of the space for lease.

As-built drawing

A drawing of a building's existing systems and components, as they are observed and documented in the field.

In addition, carry a pager or cell phone when you are away from the office so your staff can reach you immediately. In the event that you are not available, be sure your staff knows to do the following:

- Get the person's name, company name, and current location.
- Ask for a business card.
- Make an appointment for the person to meet with you. (This is a good tactic because even if you cannot make it, you now have an opportunity to call the person back and establish a personal relationship.)
- Make sure to have building brochures available at the receptionist's desk.

Other questions you and your staff should ask include:

- Is the person working with an outside broker?
- Why is the person looking for space?
- How much space does the person need?
- When does the person need the space?

Above all, never let anyone quote a rental rate, concessions, or any terms of a lease to a walk-in inquiry.

What are phone inquiries?

This type of inquiry occurs more often than the walk-in. Your strategy should be to get this person in for a tour of the building. Three important things to remember when speaking with a new prospect on the phone are:

- do not be too aggressive
- listen carefully to what the person tells you
- be patient

Often a prospect will see your phone number on a building site sign and will call about space. If you are not available, ask your staff to follow the same procedure that is used with a walk-in.

At the beginning of every conversation, fully introduce yourself and ask for the person's name, company name, and position held in the company. If the position sounds like a lower level job (the person may be a scout assigned to gather information), find out the name and contact information of the decision maker.

If the conversation begins with a request for a rental rate quote, do not quote one. Chances are that if you answer the question directly, the caller may hang up before you know who it is. (If that happens, try the *69 callback feature offered by some local phone companies.) Losing the opportunity to get prospective tenants into the building eliminates your chance to discuss your price in person, using the comparative rent grid you have developed. If the person making the phone inquiry is from another state and is unable to visit the property right away, quote a ballpark rent rate for the space.

Rent grid

A rent grid is a spreadsheet used to compare and analyze rental levels and amenities among competing properties. These grids can be used to compare any property characteristics, but are most often used to display and adjust rental rate comparisons.

What is networking?

Networking is the exchange of information or services among individuals, groups, or institutions. In other words, it is talking to others and learning what they want and need. One way to get to know the right people is to plug into your community. This is fun work, involving activities such as:

- playing golf or other athletic activities with business owners and managers
- attending appropriate civic meetings (including planning commissions, zoning boards, and chamber of commerce meetings)
- joining social organizations
- serving on charity organization committees

When you attend these functions, introduce yourself to people and ask if they know of anyone who is thinking of making an office move. Eventually, you will hear a key piece of gossip, get a tip, or obtain the inside information on events that impact the leasing market. Follow up on any clue that you pick up, regardless of the vagueness of the lead.

When you do get a prospect by networking, do not forget to thank the source. You may pay a referral fee or, if laws prohibit this kind of activity, thank that person in some other appropriate way.

What is canvassing?

Canvassing is the process of going to the offices of all of the tenants in a building, regardless of size, and, if possible, learning their lease expiration date and getting them to think about leasing space in your building. When canvassing, begin at the top floor of a building and work your way down, floor by floor.

Canvassing is time consuming and may produce few—if any—hot prospects. Other drawbacks to this sales technique include:

- being stopped by lobby security if you do not have specific business in the building
- being thrown out if people complain about unauthorized soliciting
- having receptionists refuse to open the office door for you if you do not have an appointment

When canvassing, start with buildings across the street from your building and work outward. (You have a greater chance of success with tenants located within your own neighborhood.)

The goal of canvassing is to reach the executive responsible for leasing space for the company. In between you and your target are layers of office workers. Understandably, office workers do not like to deal with a constant parade of salespeople who take up their time and distract them from doing their job.

When canvassing, you should be:

- very well groomed
- smartly dressed
- professional and pleasant

The timing of your canvassing is also important. You might want to make the calls between 2:00 PM and 4:30 PM. While this does not guarantee success, at least you will not be competing for attention during the morning rush.

What is cold-calling?

Cold-calling is a targeted process of identifying a potential prospect and then contacting that person either by phone or in person. This may appear to be the same as canvassing, but it is not. Canvassing requires you to make a physical survey of a building or area in the hopes that you might stumble upon a prospective tenant. Cold-calling is more refined: You identify the business or individuals through research and contact them. Some tips on cold-calling are:

- As with canvassing, start with businesses within a few blocks of your building and work outward.
- Make a list of companies to contact by using the research resources such as those used for creating a marketing plan.
- Before cold-calling, get organized and do some homework. Know something about the companies you will be visiting.
- Making cold calls in person is expensive compared to the efficiency of making phone calls from the office. By visiting people, however, you can learn more about each company through observing things that may provide insight into the company's leasing needs.

- Generally, it is a good idea to alternate days of outside cold-calling with days of inside phone calls. Make sure to follow up your outside calls with phone calls within a few days.

- When you choose companies to cold-call, remember that the majority of new tenants will probably come from within a three-mile radius.

- Identify the prospects on your list that are located in the same building so you can maximize your time by visiting several people in the same building. If one of these calls develops into a potential tenant, you can use that information when making other calls in that building to create momentum.

Refer to the following checklist as you research tenant prospects.

Sample Checklist for Prospecting Tenants

Tenant Referrals

_____ get the word out to current tenants

_____ offer a prize

Walk-ins

_____ keep space constantly in good condition

_____ have plans available

_____ get information from the prospect

_____ train staff to handle inquires if you're not there

Phone Inquiries

_____ listen carefully, getting name, company, and phone number

_____ avoid quoting rates

_____ get detailed information about the caller's leasing needs

_____ make an appointment to show the space

Networking

_____ become active in the community

_____ follow up on all leads

_____ thank the source when you get a prospect

Canvassing

_____ find out expiration dates of all leases in a target building

_____ learn the building's weaknesses

_____ make repeat calls to the tenants

Cold-Calling

_____ start prospecting close to your building and work outward

_____ list companies identified during research for marketing plan

_____ bring everything you need on the call such as brochures and sets of reduced floor plans

_____ dress appropriately

_____ speak to the decision maker

_____ follow up with a phone call within a few days

Brokerage Firm

_____ identify brokerage firms with the best reputations

_____ solicit written proposals

_____ review marketing materials such as brochures and direct mailings

What are the pitfalls of involving a third party?

As you work with a prospective tenant on space needs, you will develop a relationship based on respect for each other's decision-making abilities. You must be the prospect's sole contact during the preliminary stages of negotiations. The more knowledgeable you are about your product and the more you demonstrate that you want this tenant in your building, the more the prospect will see you as the person with whom to strike a deal. This gives you a certain amount of control over the outcome of the deal.

Bringing a third party into the middle of this relationship may be unacceptable to the prospective tenant and cause problems. Therefore, know the limits of your authority and what kind of deal you can make without someone else being directly involved.

To reduce third-party involvement, ask the owner to authorize you to make a deal based upon what the two of you consider market conditions. For example, if your competition is offering four months of free rent, you should be authorized to make the same concession without having to get authorization. If your asking rate has some room for reduction, you should have the ability to grant it if the tenant asks. This does not mean you have the authority to volunteer these concessions, but it does give you some negotiating strength.

FYI

A good way to keep the tenant's focus on you as the deal maker is to make the concessions within your authorized limits, but remind the prospect periodically that your decision is subject to the owner's or—even better—lender's approval. This gives you a way out just in case. Larger corporate tenants will sometimes use this same tactic by saying that the deal is subject to their superior's approval.

Making the Sale

How do I avoid quoting a price too early in a phone conversation?

Make it clear that you cannot quote a price until you know the cost of making the deal (for example, how much the tenant improvements or other concessions cost). If the person continues to press for a price, you may have to answer. However, you should make it clear that any quoted rates are subject to deal-specific adjustments to account for potential concessions, such as:

- improvements
- reimbursement for moving expenses
- extension or expansion options

FYI

Be wary of prospects who want to know the price too early. In many cases, current tenants will enter into the marketplace to shop for deals merely to be sure that the renewal they have been offered is a fair deal. This is especially true when a prospect continues to press you to disclose the rental rate without asking about any of the building's features. The prospect who does not press you about price during the first phone conversation or meeting most likely has a sincere desire to move and is the one you should pursue.

What questions should I ask during a phone inquiry?

When speaking with a prospect making a phone inquiry, you should find out as much as you can about the person and their leasing needs before you answer any questions about price. This usually requires some give and take of information. If he or she is persistent about wanting to know the price, then try this tactic: Tell the prospect you may have a few office suites available and would need to know some additional information before discussing rates, such as:

- **How much space is needed**? This helps you learn how big a deal this may become. Obviously, large space needs may cause the building's ownership to be a little more flexible than in a small deal.
- **What configuration of space is required**? This question helps you learn how much work is required to adapt the space to the prospect's needs.
- **When is the space needed**? This question can help you figure out space availability based on expiring leases.
- **Why is the person looking for space**? This important question helps you learn the motivation behind the call.
- **What is the person's present location**? This not only reveals the distance, it also indicates whether the tenant is moving upscale or downscale.

- **What is this person's business type**? Certain businesses may not be compatible or desirable. Now is the time to find out.

- **What will the space be used for? Will it be administrative, sales, storage, or some other type of use**? Again, certain uses may not be compatible or desirable.

When asking questions, be subtle and try not to act like a detective grilling a suspect. Take it slow and work the key questions into a conversation.

The purpose of learning the answers to these questions is to help craft a solution to the prospect's space needs. If the person does not want to answer some questions, pursue another line of conversation until you can backtrack. During the process, you are also sizing up the prospect and determining if he or she meets the building owner's criteria for a suitable tenant.

Once you have gotten as much information as possible, all the while explaining the building's amenities and features, ask for an appointment to show it. Be direct. Avoid posing a question like, "Would you like to see the building?" It leaves room for a prospect to back out. Instead, say something like: "I would like to show you the building. What time would be convenient?"

How do I assess a competitor's space to help me canvass effectively?

Once inside a competitor's building, your strategy should be to look for aspects that do not meet your standards and use those as sales points for your property. When touring the building, do the following:

- Examine the building's common areas, lobby, elevator cabs, and light fixtures for signs of poor maintenance and obsolescence. Note the number of elevators and if their speed can adequately accommodate heavy traffic during daily rush hours.
- Check a few restrooms. Cost cutting in building operations is most apparent in the restrooms. Note if they are properly maintained, and check the quality of the paper products and soap dispensers.
- When you enter an office suite, pay attention to the maintenance, paint job, lighting, and image portrayed in the rental space. This is another opportunity for you to find weaknesses in the competition and create sales points.
- When you are waiting to see the decision maker, ask the receptionist or secretary if the air conditioning is adequate (a common tenant complaint is poor, unreliable heating, ventilation, and air conditioning) and if there is

enough parking. Use these as conversation starters; in the event the receptionist reveals the building's inadequacies, listen carefully, and identify issues to discuss with the decision maker.

- Find out if the space you are touring is the only space that the tenant occupies in that building to determine whether the tenant had to expand to other areas of the building not next to the original space. If that is the case, you can discuss the inefficiencies of this expansion with the decision maker.

FYI

During your canvassing you will discover some weaknesses in buildings that you can use to your advantage when calling on the tenants. You should look for those same weaknesses in your own building. If you do not learn anything else in your efforts, you will at least be able to identify the adjustments you should make to keep your building from being canvassed successfully in the same manner. You may also learn new tricks to keep competitors from canvassing your building (tightened security, perhaps).

Why are repetition and follow-up important after canvassing?

After canvassing a building, make a repeat call to speak with tenants you missed or to meet with the decision makers who expressed some interest in moving. If it takes 5, 10, or 20 calls to get an appointment with a person who eventually develops into a hot prospect, it will be worth the effort.

If someone does express an interest, work fast. Get them into your building for a showing. If too much time elapses, the prospect's interest may wane.

What should I bring when going on a cold call?

- Plenty of brochures and business cards. You should give every person you meet a brochure. It may be wasted on some people, but you can use it as a prop to start a conversation.
- Sets of reduced floor plans and lists of vacant spaces to leave with the prospect if they are requested. The value of these as a sales tool should not be underestimated. Often, prospects will look at a floor plan and begin to mentally arrange the space to suit their needs.
- A calculator and a spreadsheet with relevant space data. Numbers will enter into the discussion many times, perhaps as a question about the square footage, the rental rate, or the effective rate.
- Presentation tools, such as a computer and any charts or drawings. Visual aids are invaluable to any successful sales pitch.
- Cell phone and/or pager so the office can contact you. These are not only necessities, they are also important tools that allow you to be more productive.

✦ If you like gadgets, a PDA (personal digital assistant), can be helpful. You can enter contact data into it and later download that information to a computer. Otherwise, make sure to bring along pen and paper.

If you have a CD-ROM presentation using 3D walk-through software, make sure your laptop is fully charged and everything is in working order. Always take along a spare battery as backup. When doing this type of presentation, create a macro key set-up with quick scripting that launches the presentation quickly rather than having to waste time manually keystroking your way into it. If your computer freezes or crashes, be prepared to abandon it as a presentation tool and use the printed materials.

Before you walk out the door, take a good look at yourself. A prospective tenant has too many reasons to reject your call; one of them should not be your personal appearance.

How do I reach the decision maker when cold-calling?

Ask for the decision maker by name as you enter the office of a prospective tenant. The first resistance you may encounter will be from the receptionist. He or she may demand that you have an appointment. Usually, you do not have one—yet. Ask to make the appointment at the time of your visit.

If you make it past the receptionist, your next hurdle is the decision maker's assistant. If you are rejected by the assistant, persist in your goal to speak with the decision maker. If it does not look like that is going to happen, put your offer into the form of a letter. A letter is ideal because it opens the door for you to make follow-up calls, either by phone or in person, to see if you can actually speak with the decision maker.

If you do speak to the decision maker, try to find out quickly if the company is interested in any of the following possibilities:

- new space
- consolidating space
- lowering operating expenses
- improving location

If the answer to these questions is "no," do not be discouraged. The company may develop an interest in the future. Therefore you should:

- ✦ Attempt to learn when the current lease expires.
- ✦ Maintain contact with follow-up letters every month or so. (Contact management software can be very useful when trying to keep track of follow-ups.)
- ✦ Keep up on news developments about the company. A big sale or increased earnings may create a need for the company to expand.

How many cold calls will I (or my sales team) need to make?

Say you make 10 cold calls a day, and you develop one potential prospect. In one week you will have made 50 cold calls and developed 5 prospects. From those 5 prospects you should be able to develop one good potential tenant. By making 200 calls a month, you could develop 4 strong possible tenants.

Remember that these are estimates, and much will depend on leasing activity in your area. In small markets 1 out of 100 calls often turns into a deal, which may take three months to close.

The chances of closing deals with all 4 potential tenants are slim. Usually, the best you can hope for is to close 1 out of the 4. That is 1 deal a month. Can you, or your leasing agents, survive on earnings from 1 sale a month? If not, then 10 cold calls a day may not be sufficient. If you double your cold-calling, you could double your production. The more calls made, the more chances of increasing earnings.

Is it better to cold-call prospects by phone or in person?

Some leasing agents say the phone helps them reach more people and convey their message more quickly. Others think the telephone gives the person on the other end of the line the opportunity to ignore your call, ask for you to call back, or quickly tell you they are not interested.

Busy corporate executives may be slightly less pressed to turn away someone who is calling on them in person. If you are turned away the first time, do not give up. If you keep coming back, your odds will increase because the prospect and his or her receptionist will become familiar with you. Sooner or later you may be invited in to make your sales pitch.

How do I learn what is important to the prospect?

To learn the prospect's negotiating position, listen closely to what is being said. Take mental notes about what the prospect considers the key elements of the deal. Some of the items the prospect mentions may be desirable, but not fundamental, to the transaction.

From time to time, test the reliability and ranking of importance of those key elements by repeating them to the prospect at a later date. If the prospect indicates that he or she wants, but does not really need, a certain concession, you will have an idea of how much of a priority it is.

Why should I understand a prospect's motives?

One of the most fundamental techniques of sales is to learn the prospect's motivation. Your most important tool for discovering that motivation is to listen and ask subtle questions.

For example, find out why he or she is interested in moving. If prospects tell you that they are moving because they have to, or need to, you will know that they are definitely interested in moving. If they say that they are moving because they ought to or would like to, you will know that the prospects are not that motivated and may be just casually shopping.

Never initiate a sales pitch with preplanned statements you intend to make without regard for the prospect's needs.

How should I convey that my building can satisfy the prospect's needs?

Once you understand the prospect's motivations, you should emphasize the features of your building that will satisfy the prospect's identified needs. Keep reminding the prospect that these features could be the solution to his or her problem.

Selling the other features of your building is also important. So as each part of your presentation unfolds, watch for a reaction. If you hear or see a positive response to something you said, offer more details. Do not waste time on a particular feature if there is no interest in it.

Take notes on the prospect's interests so you do not confuse one prospect's motivations with another's. Because prospects like to think they are getting individual attention, keep their comments close at hand so you can be specific when they call.

What should I remember when showing the space?

Presenting your building and the proposed space in a favorable light requires a plan of action. This plan not only keeps the prospective tenant—and you—focused, it also provides a cohesive picture of what you can offer the tenant.

When meeting with a prospective tenant to present the property, be aware of the following:

- ✦ Know the prospective tenant's needs and concerns; listen and ask clarifying questions.
- ✦ Have professional presentation materials (that is, brochures, floor plans, charts, overheads, etc.) ready.
- ✦ Walk through the space, point out features and amenities, and elicit responses; space does not show itself.

The immediate goal for walk-ins, phone inquiries, networking, canvassing, and cold-calling is to get a prospect to come in and look at your space. There will probably be an initial walk-through, followed by a more detailed one after you have submitted a proposal or had preliminary lease term discussions.

FYI

If you are showing space that is still occupied by a tenant with an expiring lease, you will need permission from the tenant to show it. This is a legal issue. Permission to enter a tenant's office suite is usually expressly granted in a specific lease clause giving access during some point in the lease term for the purpose of showing the space. Read the tenant's lease to find out when you may inspect the space and what notice you must give to do so.

How should I use presentation materials when showing a space?

While the prospective tenant may already have the building brochures and floor plans, your initial meeting is a good time to use presentation materials as you present the building both as a whole and as a backdrop for the available space. Be sure your presentation materials are well-organized and attractive; this gives the impression that you are well acquainted with all aspects of the building. Use an easel or similar presentation device to show floor plans. If using a computer, make sure everything is running properly so no embarrassing glitches or failures occur during the presentation.

In the preliminary meeting presentation with the prospect, provide the basic facts about the building and the available space. The better informed your prospect is about your building, the easier it will be for him or her to articulate specific concerns and needs. Have copies of the presentation materials conveniently packaged and available for the prospect to keep and use both during the presentation and afterward. However, do not overload prospects with too much paper—you do not want to distract them from listening to you.

How do I create a strategy for showing a space?

Before you show any space to a prospective tenant, it is wise to do a walk-through by yourself so you are familiar with:

- the space and what it offers
- its location in the building
- its relation to building services and amenities

Try to look at the space through the eyes of the prospective tenant. Once you have performed your own preliminary walk-through, make a plan to show the space. This plan should include:

- a pre-walk-through
- a walk-through with the prospective tenant
- a follow-up meeting
- a report of the feedback from the showing to the building owner

What is a pre-walk-through?

The leasing staff and property management staff usually conduct a pre-walk-through prior to the walk-through. During your pre-walk-through, make sure the space is clean and orderly. Open the blinds and turn on the lights and air conditioning to enhance the presentation. Do your pre-walk-through at least one hour before the showing so that if something is not in order, you will have enough time to make adjustments.

How do I conduct a walk-through?

During the walk-through, you should:

- Be prepared to answer as many questions as possible about the space during the walk-through.
- Guide the prospect through the space, pointing out the positive features, especially those that meet their needs and that help solve problems they are having with their existing space.
- Ask for comments about the space and allow the prospect to make his or her own observations. These observations are helpful not only in gaining further insight into the prospect's perspective, but also in presenting the space to other prospects.

- Allow plenty of time for the prospect to look at the space and explore it in depth. The prospect may bring a space planner or a team of designers who may want to make another appointment to look at the space in further detail.

Prospects or their representatives should be on time, but delays do occur. Almost every broker or decision maker carries a cell phone, so you should get a call if he or she will be late. If you do not get a call, wait half an hour before leaving.

What features should I highlight during the walk-through?

When you conduct a showing, point out all of the features of the building—not just the rental space. If your building has covered parking, show the parking and mention the benefits of having a snow-free car in the winter and a cool car in the summer. Decision makers are not going to lease space in your building just to obtain covered parking, but it may be the feature that wins you the deal.

If your HVAC system is in good shape, providing good air quality, mention it to the prospect. After all, a building that offers a quality and cost-effective environment is very attractive.

In older buildings it is important to disclose any known or possible asbestos that might cause problems when it comes time to install any tenant improvements. If your building is asbestos-free, this is an important factor to point out.

Why is it important to understand the tenant's needs and concerns?

Understanding the needs and concerns of a prospective tenant is an effective leasing tool. If you have a clear understanding of the prospect's needs before you show the space, you can avoid showing an unsuitable space and potentially losing the tenant. Keep in mind, however, that as you show the space, you will gain further insight into the prospect's requirements and concerns. Some prospects may not recognize some of their own needs and concerns until they walk through the space. Answering questions and listening carefully as you make your presentation can help define the needs and interest level. Also, whenever possible, visit the prospect's existing space to better understand his or her current situation and use that to explain how your space may improve operation.

How should I handle the follow-up meeting?

The follow-up meeting should be conducted immediately after you have shown the space, while it is fresh on the prospective tenant's mind. The follow-up may occur either in the space or, preferably, in the leasing office. The follow-up meeting gives you the opportunity to:

- respond to the prospective tenant's concerns
- assess his or her interest level
- reiterate the building's positive features

If concerns are raised, you have an opportunity to address them. If the tenant raises unreasonable or immaterial concerns, you may decide that this prospect may be unsuitable or potentially problematic.

If you do not get the chance to have a follow-up meeting in your office, try to get feedback a day or two later by calling the prospect or the prospect's agent. If that person is unavailable, leave your number. It is considered common courtesy for all tenant representatives to return calls to the showing agent.

What should I report back to the owner after a walk-through and follow-up?

Soon after the walk-through and follow-up meeting, report feedback to the owner both formally (written) and informally (verbal). If the prospect raises concerns, bring these concerns to the owner's attention. If, for example, a prospect notices evidence of a leak, find a way to correct the problem as quickly as possible. However, if a prospective tenant voices only frivolous concerns and may not be desirable, convey this issue to the owner.

How do I tell when a prospect is inclined to make a deal?

A prospective tenant who is sold on the features of the building will be motivated to complete the transaction. But the prospect may withhold this information from you until later in the negotiations. Your job is to subtly seek out any information that indicates the prospect is inclined to make a deal.

You can listen for clues regarding the prospective tenant's intention. Perhaps the prospect's office manager knows about relocating to your building, or the prospect may have talked to a transport company about getting a bid on moving. These clues are a good indication that a potential deal is progressing well. If none of these clues is evident, then it's time to ask the potential tenant questions that will give you an idea of his or her position regarding your building. Examples of these types of questions include:

- Have you inquired about telephone service and phone book listings?
- Do you anticipate any difficulty in getting your employees to accept a new location?
- Can I give you neighborhood amenity and transit maps to hand out to your employees?
- When will you begin to have mail forwarded?
- Would you like me to drop off a postal change-of-address package?
- Have you started accepting printers' bids for new stationery?

These questions can be worked into general conversation with the prospect or an employee (depending on circumstances). Try not to be too obvious because some people might perceive you as pushy or nosy.

The best indicator of a prospect's intention is getting a written commitment, such as a letter of intent or an offer to lease. These give you a more formal commitment, showing that the prospect is serious about leasing space after successful negotiations.

How do I close the sale?

Closing means making the sale. The sale is generally considered a done deal when the prospect signs a letter of intent committing to the space. Of course, to be fully closed and for the leasing agent to earn a commission, the prospective tenant must sign a lease. Because the time period between identifying a prospect and signing the lease can be long, sometimes it may take an opener and a closer to bring in a deal (which may mean a split commission).

Close the transaction as quickly as possible. The prospect's reason for moving gives you a clue as to whether to push for a quick closing or back off and not press too much. If the prospect is not ready to close right away, an alternative is to get him or her to sign a letter of intent, or a letter of interest in the space.

If the prospect is moving because a larger tenant in the next suite is going to expand and wants the prospect's present space, you know that time is a factor and a quick decision is required. Therefore, you can press harder for a quick sale. On the other hand, if there does not appear to be any significant reason for the move, you should not press the prospect into a sale, and therefore, a soft close is more likely.

Soft close

Backing off and not pressing as much during real estate dealings.

No one can close a sale without asking for the order, so you should tell prospects that you want their business and ask for it. You will need to learn how to be aggressive, but not so aggressive that you lose the sale.

Lease Negotiation Strategies and Tactics

Why is it important to know a little psychology during negotiations?

Sales negotiations involve more than the give and take over the terms and conditions of a lease. A lot more is going on: personality issues, posturing, one-upmanship, fear, and greed. These complex issues affect both the people doing the negotiating and attributes of the product being negotiated. Sometimes the personalities of the negotiators have more bearing on the success of the deal than the business terms.

Psychological characteristics seep into every negotiation. These dynamics begin at the first moment of contact. For example, your answer to a simple question about the amount of space can set the tone for further discussions. Even before you get to answer that question, the prospect has begun formulating an opinion of you and your organization. This impression starts when the receptionist answers the phone and is influenced by how long he or she put the prospect on hold and the tone of your voice when you finally answered—was it warm and cheery, or tired and bored?

Your answers to the prospect's questions add more layers to this impression. If you are at all ambiguous in your responses, the prospect may think you are not interested in what you are selling. For example, saying, "I think it's around 2,000 square feet," instead of a definite "2,000 square feet," will convey your lack of knowledge and initiative. If you make an error, you can correct it later. But sounding like you do not know what you are selling puts you at an immediate disadvantage.

What are some helpful negotiation strategies and tactics?

Create a strategy to negotiate terms and conditions for a lease when you know the prospect is truly interested in the space. By this time, you may have agreed on the easy things and need to move on to items that require negotiation. Some of these issues may turn out to be deal breakers. To get through these negotiations in a good position, use the following tactics:

- brinkmanship
- straw man theory
- faceless-manager approach
- lender-approval-needed approach

What is brinkmanship?

Brinkmanship is a "take it or leave it" tactic. As your negotiations proceed, there are bound to be a few issues on both sides of the table that can sink the deal, because neither side wants to give in. The prospect will tell you that unless you agree to a certain point, he or she will walk away from the deal. If you refuse to agree to the request, you are bringing the deal to the brink, which is why this tactic is called brinkmanship.

If you use this tactic, (make sure to clear it first with the building owner), you must be very sure of yourself and know for a fact that even if the prospect does not get his or her way, you will still get the deal. In a soft market brinkmanship can be a dangerous gamble, because the tenant has too many other attractive alternatives. One way to handle this situation is to discuss other terms of the transaction and return to the difficult one later. If there is still an impasse on the key issues, adjourn the meeting and resume when both of you have had time to assess the consequences.

If you believe the deal is in serious jeopardy, immediately consult with the building owner to see how flexible he or she is on this issue. If a legal or insurance issue is involved, then you may need to speak with the owner's attorney to see if you can work out an acceptable alternative.

What is straw man theory?

In some negotiating you may want to seize on an unimportant issue and make it seem important. This strategy is called the straw man theory, because it is like a scarecrow in the cornfield that appears to be something it is not. The goal is to distract the prospect from concentrating too much on all the terms of the deal. Never use this tactic in the beginning of negotiations.

This strategy requires convincing acting. The following are some tips for creating a straw man.

- Do not concede anything that is important to the owner.
- Choose something that is not of major importance to you and make it a big deal (it becomes your straw man).
- Create the illusion that this issue is important.
- Let the issue materialize during discussions, especially if negotiations are getting hung up.
- Try to be spontaneous about your straw man issues, but do not overact.
- To find straw man issues, listen to what prospects say during interactions and find a few things they need that will not cost you much to offer.

- Make a big show of how hard it is for you to make the concession.
- Make the prospects work to get what they want.

What is the faceless-manager approach?

If you have ever sat at a car salesperson's desk and had him or her leave the room to get your deal approved by a manager in the back room, you are familiar with the faceless-manager negotiating tactic. If you are the person responsible for leasing the space and have the authority to make a deal, do not divulge this information to your prospective tenant. Most of the time, you should claim that someone with more authority will need to approve the transaction.

Most prospects will want to cut the best deal possible and will strive to get you to offer concessions such as lower rent. This is when someone else of authority can be helpful: you can tell the prospect, "Well, let's see if this will fly." Bring the offer to the owner (or just leave the room for a while), and return with a counter offer on that one issue.

To use the faceless-manager approach effectively, you must understand which terms and conditions the real owner will concede. Also, remember that you will rarely make a deal that fits all of the parameters you have been given. Therefore, you must have access to the owner or the person who represents the owner so that you can quickly get answers about how much flexibility you have.

FYI

In certain situations the faceless-manager approach can backfire. When involving an owner in negotiations, decision making can become convoluted at best, and indecisive at worst. For you, the danger is in losing control of the deal as you become a messenger between the owner and prospect.

To make the faceless-manager approach work, you must:

- Establish guidelines (preferably in the form of a memo), backed by the owner or final decision maker.
- Have immediate access to the owner or final decision maker. (This is when cell phone contact is critical.)
- Be ready at decision time, because few prospects will wait if you're not.

What is the lender-approval-needed approach?

This tactic is similar to the faceless-manager approach. If the agreement for the mortgage on your building requires the lender to approve each deal, you must know what the lender will approve. Learn these parameters when you accept a sales position.

If the lender needs to approve every deal, you can divulge this in the beginning of any serious negotiations. You might also hold this information back and use it later when you get to a term that you know is not going to be approved. Then you can say that you will need to run it by the lender.

If written documents, such as a proposal or letter of intent, are involved, these documents must state that the lease terms are subject to lender approval.

It is critical, however, that you are certain the turnaround time for lender approval is going to be reasonable. Since it may have to move through several layers of bureaucracy, you may want to learn how many departments are part of the review process.

If the lender has final say so, you need to be able to communicate with the person at the lending institution who makes this decision. Learn who this person is, and take him or her out to lunch to establish a personal rapport if you can. This way, when a tight deal comes along that may be at the limits of lender acceptability, you might be able to informally present the terms to this person and get a feel if he or she will accept them before you formally submit them.

FYI

Never let it appear that you are trying to run the lender's approval process. What you are trying to do is save everyone from wasting time on a dead-end deal.

The requirement of lender approval may also give you another negotiating strategy because you can claim the lender will not approve an unreasonable demand. If you divulge at the beginning of negotiations that the lender must approve everything, you cannot use this tactic.

What documents are used during negotiations?

Negotiations with commercial tenants usually require a variety of documents. As burdensome as all this paperwork can become, it also makes it easier to organize and address the many issues that must be integrated into a lease document.

The basic negotiating documents include:

- RFP (request for proposal)
- proposal
- broker's comparison sheet
- letter of intent
- offer to lease

Being asked for a proposal or offering to provide a letter of intent is a significant step in the negotiating process.

No hard-and-fast rule covers the information these preliminary documents should contain or the format they should follow. But always ask an experienced commercial real estate attorney to review these documents to make sure you do not say or imply something that may become a problem when the lease is being drafted. These issues may be grounds for a lawsuit if negotiations fall apart.

The lease is the binding document, but before it is signed, it is a good idea to have all written communications briefly state that none of the proposed terms and conditions are binding on either party until the lease is signed.

FYI

You may become frustrated if the prospect brings a lawyer to the table early in the negotiations. At the beginning of negotiations, discuss business terms of the lease such as rent, additional rent, expenses, term, and renewals. If the prospect brings a lawyer into negotiations at this stage, the lawyer may cloud communication. This situation may force you to bring in your attorney to talk to their attorney, cutting both primary parties out of the discussions.

What is an RFP (request for proposal)?

The RFP is the document the broker representing a tenant sends to building owners to generate a proposal. It lists certain needs and requirements of the prospect and requests a proposal from those building owners who can meet those needs. A formal RFP may be issued when an outside broker is representing a tenant (see the sample tenant RFP form on the following pages). RFPs are also issued by government agencies; the largest is the General Services Administration of the federal government. As part of the RFP process, the entity requesting the proposal from you may provide an outline of requirements and specifications that you must meet before the prospect will even consider the space.

Sample Tenant RFP Form

Tenant Request for Proposal
Space in Corporate Towers
0000 Corporate Boulevard
Major City, Any State 00000-0000

Premises:	Suite 100
Area:	Approximately 10,000 rentable ft^2 (rentable area may not include more than a 15% common area factor).
Lease Term:	Sixty-three (63) months
Occupancy:	Not later than January 1, 2006
Base Rental Rate:	\$0.00 per rentable ft^2 months 1-6 \$17.00 per rentable ft^2 months 7-12 \$17.50 per rentable ft^2 months 13-24 \$18.00 per rentable ft^2 months 25-48 \$18.60 per rentable ft^2 months 49-63
Operating Expenses & Real Estate Taxes:	Tenant shall be responsible for its pro rata share of operating expenses and real estate taxes, which are estimated at \$9.00 per rentable ft^2 annually. Controllable expenses are to be capped at 5% increase per year.
Tenant Improvements:	Tenant shall be provided a turnkey buildout in accordance with the attached plan. Please indicate the estimated cost of the proposed tenant improvements.
Architectural & Space Planning Services:	Landlord shall pay for all architectural and space planning services, including construction drawings and furniture layout plans.
Delayed Occupancy:	In the event the January 1, 2006 occupancy date is not achieved, Landlord shall be responsible for and reimburse Tenant promptly for all rent and any holdover penalties incurred by Tenant after the expiration of Tenant's current lease term.
Termination Provision:	Tenant requires a termination provision after the second year of occupancy; Tenant shall agree to pay to Landlord a sum equal to any unamortized tenant improvements expended by the Landlord on behalf of the tenant.
Hours of Operation:	Services and utilities shall be provided Monday through Friday from 7:00 a.m. to 7:00 p.m. (except holidays); after-hours air conditioning/heating shall be available in 2-hour increments at a charge not to exceed \$20.00 per hour.

Parking:	Five (5) reserved garage parking spaces shall be available to tenant at no charge throughout the term of the Lease; nonreserved open parking is available free of charge. The building ratio is four (4) cars per 1,000 ft^2 of rentable space.
Signage:	Directory signage in the lobby, signage at the entry to the leased premises, and signage on the main building pylon sign shall be provided and maintained by Landlord at Landlord's sole cost and expense.
Security Deposit:	Waived
Hazardous Materials:	Landlord shall warrant and represent that the building and land do not contain asbestos or contamination of any kind; Landlord shall also certify, by means of independent laboratory testing, that radon levels in the leased premises and common areas of the building shall not exceed 4 picocuries per liter.
Renewal Option:	Tenant requires a renewal option for an additional 60-month term at a rental rate not to exceed the lesser of the Tenant's base rental rate during the sixty-third month of the original lease of 95% of the fair market rent at the time of renewal. Within sixty (60) days of the commencement of the renewal term, Landlord shall replace all carpet within the premises, paint all painted surfaces, and contribute a reasonable renewal allowance to Tenant for reconfiguration or replacement of furniture and furniture systems.
Brokerage Commission:	Tenant warrants and represents that it has not engaged the services of a broker or brokerage firm and has dealt with no broker or brokerage firm other than Landlord's brokerage firm.

This request for proposal does not constitute an offer to lease or binding commitment on the part of Preferred Tenant Corporation. It is understood that no commitment shall exist on the part of tenant in the absence of a formal written lease agreement, properly executed by an authorized representative of Preferred Tenant Corporation. Proposals must be received no later than two (2) weeks from the date on this.letter

Respectfully Submitted,

PREFERRED TENANT CORPORATION

By__________________________ __________________________

Authorized Representative Date

Its __________________________

Sample Tenant RFP Form

Courtesy of CB Commercial Real Estate Group, Inc.

RFPs can be requested either before the tenant looks at the space or after the tenant has inspected and selected the building. Most of the time the tenant will be identified by the representing broker before the RFP is issued.

The RFP should include a statement that the tenant is interested in your property and:

- the tenant's space needs
- the timing of a proposed move
- the length of the lease
- the amount of space required

The following standard information will also be requested:

- a specific move-in date
- parking allowances
- the size and location of the space (sometimes supported by drawings)
- a commitment from the owner to pay the brokerage commission (if there is one)
- the length of the lease
- the structure of any options to renew
- the availability of expansion space
- the overall square footage of the building
- the number of stories

- an expense stop or base year to determine the tenant portion of operating expenses
- the deadline for a response
- a statement that the RFP should not be interpreted as an offer to lease

Most of the time, the RFP will require the same information that would be discussed at a negotiating table. However, sometimes other requests are listed, including:

- a moving allowance
- a copy of the building's standard lease
- free rent
- the option to take over an existing lease in exchange for payment of a higher lease rate
- other customized features of their proposed transaction

Expect an RFP to be extremely detailed. Aside from the business terms of a proposed lease, it may request information about:

- mechanical systems
- floor load weights
- electrical power
- life safety features
- disclosure of ownership

- management and staffing
- the environmental condition of the property (asbestos, toxic waste, clean air standards)
- Americans with Disabilities Act compliance, as well as all other codes and statutes
- nondiscrimination in employment and leasing

If the prospective tenant has not seen the property, and you have not met in person before responding to the RFP, you should find out the motivations of the tenant. If an outside broker is involved, ask that person about the motivations of the tenant. You can be more candid in your discussions and perhaps learn the reasons behind the specific request. Discover the major points of interest so you can emphasize ways your building could be responsive to the issues that are important to the tenant.

How do I respond to an RFP?

When responding to the RFP, answer all questions and provide the requested information. If the information must be presented in a particular format, follow that format. Lack of information, or deviation from the RFP's instructions, may cause a tenant who is looking at several properties simultaneously to rule out your building. Deliver the response before the deadline and be sure that you can deliver what you promise.

FYI

Integrity is extremely important. Get a commitment from the owner to honor the terms before you submit them. If the tenant chooses your building and you cannot deliver what was promised, not only will you lose the deal, but you will also find it harder to lease because word will get around that you cannot deliver what you promise.

The final step in your response to the RFP is to include disclaimers. These disclaimers may say that the proposal and its contents are only valid for a given period of time. Furthermore, they may state that the terms may be changed if a response is not received within the time allotted or that the building owner reserves the right to lease the space to others during the time of the offer.

FYI

Using a disclaimer allows you to offer the same space to other prospective tenants while the original prospect is making a decision. However, tenants might ask that the space be taken off the market while they consider your proposal. There is no easy answer to this problem. If you are having difficulty leasing space or the market has been extremely slow, consider honoring the request. You may also agree to this if the tenant is willing to compensate the building owner for keeping the space off the market. In most cases, though, you should not take the space off the market. There is always the possibility that another tenant may want the space.

What is included in a proposal?

The proposal is the document that you send the prospective tenant offering basic business terms and conditions. This proposal may be written before or after you show the space and indicates a serious level of negotiations. A proposal is a way to start serious lease negotiations. It is important to learn how to create sound proposals in proper form. Many real estate firms have their own formats for making proposals (see the sample proposal on the following pages).

Landlord Proposal to Lease
Corporate Towers
0000 Corporate Boulevard
Major City, Any State 00000-0000

Tenant:	Preferred Tenant Corporation
Premises:	Suite 100, consisting of approximately 10,000 rentable ft^2 (see attachment demising plan).
Occupancy:	January 1, 2006
Lease Term:	Five (5) years
Base Rental Rate:	$18 per rentable ft^2 annually, with five percent (5%) annual escalations.
Operating Expenses, Real Estate Taxes, & Insurance:	Tenant shall be responsible for its pro rata share of operating expenses, real estate taxes, and insurance on a full pass-through basis, which costs are estimated at $9.50 per rentable ft^2 annually.
Security Deposit:	Landlord requires a security deposit equal to two (2) months' base rent, operating expenses, real estate taxes, and insurance to be paid not later than the date the Lease is fully executed.
HVAC:	Services and utilities are provided Monday through Friday from 8:00 a.m. to 6:00 p.m. (except holidays); after-hours air conditioning/heating is available (with prior notice to building management) in 2-hour increments, currently charged to the Tenant at $25.00 per hour with a 2-hour minimum.
Parking:	The building parking ratio is 4 cars per 1,000 ft^2 of rentable space. Nonreserved parking is available free of charge; limited covered or reserved parking is currently available at $50.00 per month per vehicle.
Security Systems:	24-hour access is available through a card-key system.
Amenities:	Global Bank full-service branch; two cafes; one sundries shop with shoe shine/dry cleaning service available; one travel agency; one building exercise room with shower/changing rooms; select concierge services.
Landlord:	Owner Investment Corporation
Tenant Improvements:	Landlord, at its sole cost and expense, shall modify the Premises in accordance with the attached plan, using building standard materials. Any costs for additional improvements to the Premises, or deviation from the attached plan, shall be amortized over the term of the Lease at an interest rate of 12% per annum.
Brokerage Disclosure:	Pursuant to Any State/Province Statute No. 000 regarding brokerage disclosure, Tenant warrants and represents that it has dealt with no brokerage firm other than Leasing Professionals, Inc., who exclusively represents Landlord in this transaction, and Tenant agrees to indemnify Landlord from any claims of other brokerage firms relating to this transaction.

Sample Proposal

This proposal is not a legally binding contract, or a reservation of space, but merely the terms and conditions that may be incorporated into a fully executed lease document. It is also subject to Landlord's review and acceptance of Tenant's most recent financial statements and references and prior leasing.

Please acknowledge your acceptance of the above terms and conditions by having an authorized representative sign where indicated below. If this proposal is acceptable to you, it will then be submitted to the Landlord for review and acceptance. This proposal shall remain valid for a period not longer than thirty (30) days from the date hereof, after which time it shall become null and void and have no further force and effect.

Respectfully submitted,	Agreed and Accepted:
LEASING PROFESSIONALS, INC. CORPORATION	PREFERRED TENANT
By____________________ Designated Leasing Professional	By____________________
Date____________________	____________________ (Print Name)
	Its____________________

Sample Proposal
Courtsey of CB Commercial Real Estate Group, Inc.

To create your own proposal, include the following information.

- date of the proposal
- expiration date if not accepted
- location of the space
- amount of square footage, rentable or usable
- the system used to determine space measurements
- term of the lease
- timing of the move

- date of possession
- rental rate
- any economic concessions, such as free rent or additional tenant finish.
- expense stop, expense pass-through, or base year
- tenant-finish allowances and preliminary specifications
- parking allotment
- options for renewal and expansion
- disclaimers
- any information specifically requested in the RFP

Presentation is critical when preparing a proposal. All information should be presented in a way that is easy to read and understand. At the very least, develop a customized binder or folder. Include inserts of the floor plan and other informational brochures, your business card, and a detailed proposal letter. The elements of the proposal should be independent of each other, thus allowing you to make changes to one without having to change them all.

You can also include:

- color pictures (or color copies) of the exterior and interior of the building
- pictures of any special features in the building, such as a cafeteria

- maps showing the location of area amenities
- special features that are not covered by the brochure
- a list of tenants already located in the building
- information tailored to the prospect, addressing all the features important to the tenant

The proposal must create a good impression with people other than the tenant's local office manager. While the local manager may recommend the project, that person's boss must also agree. If additional layers of authority will review the proposal, ask the prospect how many there are, and send the appropriate number of folders.

FYI

Many issues are riding on your proposal, so there is no room for misspellings, misstatements of facts or figures, blurred photographs, or poor photocopies. If you are not able to produce a professional package, find someone with graphic design experience. If you are not a writer, find a person who can draft the necessary documents. Make sure to read everything twice to check for errors. Never trust the spell checker in your word processor to catch grammar and usage errors. Someone who can read the document with fresh eyes should do the final proofreading.

What is a broker's comparison sheet?

A broker's comparison sheet enables a tenant to compare your building with others. A comparison sheet can be used as both a marketing tool and a negotiating tactic to help you sell your building.

A prospective tenant can get confused when looking at several buildings and forget which building provided what. To avoid this confusion, a broker will typically provide the tenant with a comparison sheet, putting the key information on paper. This gives tenants the opportunity to review each of the possibilities in a logical manner.

The problem with a broker's comparison sheet is that it does not address all of the amenities that each building has to offer. Typically it covers only the key business points of each property. Sometimes this lack of information will slow the decision-making process or put your building at a disadvantage.

It is up to you to be sure that the prospect understands all of the benefits of the building. Offering the prospective tenant your own comparison sheet helps you sell your building. You can fill in the blanks with your property's strong points; the tenant fills in the blanks for competing buildings.

FYI

If you know you have an edge on your competition, a broker's comparison sheet can help tenants reach a favorable decision. Do not use this sheet if you do not have an edge.

What should a letter of intent include?

All letters should state that the terms and conditions are not binding and only those contained in a signed lease will obligate the parties. Some negotiation issues should be binding, and these must be stated. One example is an agreement of confidentiality. If the prospect gives you certain business information or you make a concession, neither of you wants to have this information divulged to anyone else. Other examples are agreements stating that the prospect will not look at other space or the owner will not negotiate with another prospect for the space.

In a strong market, the prospective tenant usually gives the letter of intent to the owner. This is often done when the prospect is concerned that the landlord may reach an agreement with another prospect and wants to assert that he or she is serious about leasing the space. The prospect may also provide a letter of intent when he or she wants to secure a specific location in the building and wants the landlord to take the space off the market until the parties can reach a formal agreement.

In a soft market, the owner will often use the letter of intent as a negotiating strategy to get a commitment from a prospective tenant and to stop the tenant from pursuing other spaces.

In a tight market, the letter of intent could also require the tenant to post a deposit or to pay for space-planning costs, should the tenant withdraw from negotiations.

The owner might also use a letter of intent to line up financing for a new building or to refinance an older one.

For the letter of intent to reflect the intention of all parties, both sides must sign the letter. Of course, if either party does not like the contents of the letter, he or she could make modifications, initial the changes, and return the letter for acceptance. Usually it is best to discuss objections with the prospect before modifying the letter. Otherwise, you may look foolish if you make counteroffers the tenant will not accept.

What is an offer to lease?

An offer to lease is a variation on the letter of intent. While it cites the business terms of the proposed lease, it is a formal offer and may be subject to the interpretation of the offer and acceptance laws of the state in which the building is located. After the offer to lease is countersigned by the owner, it may become binding on both parties.

As with letters of intent, certain legal technicalities pertain to offers to lease. Before writing or accepting one, have an attorney review it.

Leasing Retail Space

Should I lease retail space in an office building?

The majority of office buildings constructed today have some type of retail space. Besides generating better rents than office space, retail space offers your tenants convenient goods and services. In addition, a building's retail space is part of the curb appeal, a factor in a prospect's evaluation process. A variety of stores in a retail area is a benefit that can help prospects choose your building over the competition.

Curb appeal

The appeal of the exterior of a rental property.

When evaluating options for creating retail space, make sure to look beyond the first floor lobby. Retail space can be almost anywhere—from a basement gym to a top-floor restaurant. Some office buildings have even integrated residential space such as apartments and hotels. When it comes to developing retail leasing opportunities, think creatively.

What are the different types of retail space?

There are five basic categories, or sizes, of inside retail space:

- mall
- arcade
- kiosk
- special-use
- pad

What is mall space?

Mall space is usually in the first floor lobby and leased to larger users who need doorways to the street and the interior of the building. Don't confuse the term mall space with the term suburban shopping mall space.

Mall space can contain several businesses, including quick print shops, dry cleaners, and coffee shops. Stores in a mall space may have direct access to the street of a shopping district. The difference between mall and arcade space is the size and location of the rental unit. Mall space generally has greater depth and requires a tenant who needs a larger space.

If your office building is connected to an enclosed central shopping mall, coordinate with the person leasing the shopping mall, particularly regarding tenant mix. Do not make the mistake of leasing space in your office building mall to the same type of store located a few feet away in the shopping mall. In addition, you will need to:

- be aware of foot traffic patterns
- be conscious of shared security concerns
- know the individual store operators
- be aware of deliveries and trash removal times

FYI

Most of the time, tenants in office building mall space are part of a local, regional, or national chain. This type of tenant is usually charged a fixed minimum rent based on a percentage of sales. For example, rental terms may be 1,000 square feet at $15/square foot triple net and sales of 6 percent in excess of $250,000.

What is arcade space?

Arcade space can be located anywhere there is a walkway where people travel from one place to another. It can be on the ground floor, on the lower levels, or at the intersection of enclosed elevated walkways that connect buildings. An example of arcade space is the area connecting an office building to a hotel or train station. Arcade space is typically used by businesses such as newsstands, floral shops, delis, snack food shops, and travel agencies.

Arcade space is usually shallow, allowing an exceptional amount of frontage (front exposure). The frontage is often glass, and most of the time, the entryway is through sliding glass doors. These rental units are typically less than 1,000 square feet. In some cases it is better to lease this space at a set monthly rate rather than by the square foot or using a percentage rent.

This type of space should be leased on a short-term basis, such as a month-to-month lease at a flat rate. This gives the building the most control over the space and allows the building management to make changes based on styles and trends. For purposes of building financing, treat month-to-month leases as nonexistent since the income cannot be guaranteed beyond 30 days.

Leasing space month to month to a smaller retail tenant offers distinct advantages. Typically, the user will be an entrepreneur working alone, rather than part of a chain, with a smaller budget. Therefore, the tenant will be more concerned about monthly operating costs and should have a monthly rental budget in mind.

FYI

Do not get desperate and change your leasing plan if you find yourself trying to market a large amount of arcade space with few takers. Think carefully before allowing a large potential tenant to change the design or remove most of the glass frontage. The ambience of the arcade space could be lost for the existing and future tenants, and you could find yourself with more, rather than less, vacancy if the tenant is not successful.

What is kiosk space?

Kiosk space is self-contained and freestanding and may be located inside or outside the building. It is the smallest space you can lease to a retail tenant and usually does not share common walls with other tenants. Rent for this space is not calculated by square foot. Therefore, establishing rent requires flexibility. One way to set rent is to estimate the volume of sales the tenant will achieve and then reach an agreement over how much rent the tenant will pay.

If the kiosk space is in the center of a high traffic area, the rent level should be increased accordingly. If the tenant's goods or services will be a building amenity, rent will become a secondary matter.

Kiosk space can be used by entrepreneurial tenants just starting out as a step toward renting larger space. If start-up tenants are successful, you can move them to arcade or other larger space.

Kiosk space does not require the same type of detailed lease used for arcade or kiosk space. Generally, the shorter and simpler the lease paperwork, the better. A lease agreement covering the major points and basic rules should be sufficient. Instruct your lawyer to attempt to keep leases for kiosk space to about two pages.

What is special-use space?

Special-use space is earmarked for a specific type of tenant and may be located almost anywhere. Almost every office building has space that is unsuitable for traditional office use because of the design of the lobby, the entryway to the elevator systems, or other reasons. This space is attractive to retail tenants. Special-use space may be integrated into the building during its design stage.

When deciding how to use special-use space, hire a retail marketing consultant to help you determine what type of retail establishment will generate the most sales and rental income for the building owner. Once you determine the best use for the space, your leasing agents will know the types of businesses to target. Typical special-use space tenants include:

- cafeterias and coffee shops
- care facilities
- financial institutions
- parking facilities
- restaurants
- athletic facilities

Cafeterias and coffee shops: Depending on the size of the space, local building codes, and other regulations, a building cafeteria food court might work in special-use space.

A cafeteria or coffee shop is generally viewed as a building amenity and may not produce pro forma rent. But it can help attract large office tenants whose employees are seldom given lengthy lunch periods.

Pro forma

A financial projection of income and expense for a future period.

FYI

If you choose to place a food-court in your building, be aware of the impact on office tenants and overall security. Crowds and lines could bother office tenants, and trash and spills may present problems. Traffic from outside the building may also be attracted to your food court.

Care facilities: Care facilities in office buildings have become popular because they allow two-income couples to work. However, leasing space for care arrangements can be difficult. The tenant operator is usually subject to numerous government regulations covering facilities, specialized restrooms, drinking fountains, fire safety requirements, and so on. These requirements generally drive up the cost of the space, making it difficult for the care tenant to pay the required rent. Set-up costs for a care center may be subsidized by corporate tenants or shared with the building and treated as an operating expense or CAM (common area maintenance) charge. It may be more beneficial—for occupancy reasons—for the building to subsidize the cost of the facility rather than not to have it at all. You can subsidize by giving the care tenant a reduced rent, greater tenant improvement allowance, or both.

FYI

Before entering into any agreement to provide or lease to a care center, make sure all permits and licenses are in place, and run a background check of the care center owners and managers.

Financial institutions: Security is a major topic during lease negotiations with banks. The property manager may be faced with exterior and/or interior alterations. When deciding whether to lease space to a financial institution, keep in mind that, typically, this type of user will want a significant amount of signage outside and inside the building. Financial tenants cannot survive with only customers from within the building. Consider the effect the signage will have on the image of the building. Once a bank sign is up, your building may become linked to its name. If this is the situation, charge a higher rent. The more exposure given to the tenant, the higher the rent.

Parking facilities: If you plan to charge for parking, whether in a lot or in a multilevel garage, another special-use space tenant will be the operator (often called a contractor) of the parking facilities. Parking customers may be tenants of the building, tenants of nearby buildings, or visitors to the building. You should look for three things when evaluating candidates for this type of tenancy:

- experience at operating parking facilities
- a reputation for fair dealing and integrity
- willingness to staff and manage the facility properly during the lease period when revenues are low

Parking tenants may want the option to earn them additional revenue by offering car services. These activities might include washing the cars or teaming up with a nearby auto service garage to provide off-site service to cars—tune-ups and repairs, for instance—in the garage. These additional services could be an attractive tenant amenity for the building owner. A parking tenant will typically agree to share a percentage of the additional revenues. Most often, the percentage is based on parking income—usually between 40 and 75 percent.

Restaurants and athletic facilities: These facilities can be part of the building design, so often tenants who will operate the facilities are selected before the building is built.

What is pad space?

Pad space is outside the building. This space is at the edge of your parking area and is usually leased to freestanding fast-food chains. The building owner can also set up a deli operation in the space. Successfully leasing pad space depends on at least three factors:

- **Parking space**: You must have adequate parking for tenants of your building so you can lease any surplus space. The number of parking spaces you are required to have is often set by state or local zoning codes.
- **Location**: Pad space on a major road with adequate traffic count and signals that allow patrons from opposite lanes to turn into the space is desirable. Corner space is more sought after than space in the middle of the block.
- **Permission**: Permission from the local zoning board to build a restaurant on the land. Be aware that getting a retail-use permit on a strip of land that's been zoned for office use is often difficult.

How do I lease retail space?

The key to leasing any retail space is to have a competent operator and a steady supply of shoppers. This ensures that the business will be profitable and the space will stay leased without a high turnover of tenants. Prospective retail tenants are not usually as concerned about the amenities of your building as office tenants. They are interested in the bottom line.

The location of the space is critical to generating sales. There are generally two types of locations in retail space: downtown and suburban. In downtown business districts, retail space is at sidewalk level, with an entrance usually on the outside of the building. Suburban office building retail space, especially in sprawling multi-building office parks, is usually in a central location in each structure and caters to the tenants of the building.

How do I find the right retail tenant?

Finding the right retail tenant is similar to finding office tenants. In general, if you want to make sure you are maximizing retail opportunities in your space, hire a retail marketing consultant to advise the building owner about the types of retail businesses that would succeed in that space. Retail marketing consultants know what sells, why, and where.

Once you have this information, you will be able to ask your leasing team to focus on the right prospects. Just as you have criteria for choosing office tenants, you will need similar criteria for your retail space. Three important points to consider are:

- The retail tenant mix must provide goods and services that people would most likely purchase.
- The tenant must not duplicate either the type of store or the goods and services already available nearby.
- The people running the operation must know what they are doing.

How do I find a retail marketing consultant?

To find a retail marketing consultant, try calling the nearest university business school and ask to speak with a faculty member in the marketing department. Once you establish that you have reached the right person, explain what you need, and they may have some referrals for you. Another source is your local planning or economic development agency. They often use consultants to prepare market analysis and reports. The easiest way to find a retail marketing consultant is to ask the office leasing brokers with whom you do business.

What do I need to know about a prospective retail tenant?

Whether a prospective retail tenant responded to a "for lease" sign in your window or was brought to you by a leasing agent, you will need to know a few things about the operator and the business so you can determine whether or not it will be a good match for the building. Questions to ask include:

- **Where are the closest competing businesses**? A new location could saturate the market and dilute sales. This can happen when a national chain sells too many franchises during the early stages of its success, and competing stores begin to cannibalize sales. Ask your retail marketing consultant to create a map showing all the similar types of businesses close to your building.

- **Do the prospective retail tenants have current locations in other office buildings, and how are they doing**? Visit these other sites, and observe customer traffic, store conditions, and staff competence. Do not hesitate to ask to see proof of sales and other financials during negotiations.

- **How will the new store complement existing stores**? An attractive store will stimulate sales and encourage the owners of other stores to make their stores attractive as well. Attach some uniform signage and design rules in addition to the standard building rules to every retail lease.

- **Does the retail tenant have a good reputation**? Be sure to review references carefully. This tenant will be dealing with other building tenants on a daily basis. Their operational capabilities, the appearance of their rental space, and their treatment of your tenants will have a direct effect on the overall success of the building. If you are leasing space to a restaurant or coffee shop operator, you may want to go to the local health department or government agency that licenses food establishments. Ask if the prospect had any violations or complaints at other locations.

What do prospective retail tenants want to know?

All prospective retail tenants will want to know as much as they can about other office and retail tenants and the neighborhood. This information is most commonly called building, or area, demographics. If there is a significant amount of retail space to lease, have basic information about the tenants in the building on hand to give to retail tenants. This information should include at least the following:

- ✦ the amount of occupied building space
- ✦ the number of people in the building
- ✦ the time of their arrival
- ✦ the time the majority of tenants leave for lunch and where they eat
- ✦ the level of income
- ✦ the approximate number of male and female employees
- ✦ the approximate age of employees
- ✦ the types of work performed by the building tenants

If the space has exterior entrances, you should also have information about the neighborhood, such as foot and vehicular traffic counts. The more information you can give retail tenants about their potential customers, the more interested they will become. Usually, exterior traffic and pedestrian counts can be found at government agencies, such as city development agencies, regional planning commissions, municipal public works departments, and traffic bureaus.

How do I negotiate a retail lease?

Negotiations for retail space are quite different from negotiations for office space in that the retail tenant's perception of the space and its influence on potential sales will have a direct bearing on the amount of rent the tenant is willing to pay.

You can figure the base rent using the same approach as for determining the base rent of office space. This means performing a market survey on the amount of office retail space available in the micromarket and the current rental rates. The current value of the vacant space should be based on the supply and demand of retail space that will directly compete with retail space in your building. As usual, be cautious of the owner's expectations in obtaining the pro forma rate. Only the market survey will reveal the true value of the space. In addition, there may be the same lender requirements to meet as with your office leases.

How do I measure retail space?

Measurement of retail space is slightly different from measurement of office space. The reason for this is that retail space is usually self-contained, and the tenant of the space does not use the common areas of the building.

FYI

The subject of calculating retail store area is covered in BOMA's *Standard Method for Measuring Floor Area in Office Buildings.*

How do I price retail space?

The price of retail space is based on the sales potential of the rental space. Be flexible and don't get locked into a long-term fixed rent—retail tenants are usually willing to pay more once the location has proven itself.

One way to include sales potential as part of the lease is for the landlord and the tenant to agree that after the business is established—perhaps three or six months after opening—the tenant will pay additional rent based on a percentage of the sales generated. This allows the tenant to establish its business without having to pay a burdensome rent at a time when advertising and promotional expenses are high. If the demographics and traffic counts of the space are accurate, and the tenant's business flourishes, the tenant should be willing to pay a higher rent after business is steady.

How do I negotiate percentage rent?

To establish a percentage rent, both parties must agree on how to calculate the percentage. The best way to determine percentage rent is to agree on a volume of sales per square foot. The negotiation of sales per square foot will be difficult because the tenant will want to be conservative, and the landlord will want the percentage to reflect the predicted strength of the location.

FYI

To get a feel for the potential annual average of sales per square foot, check out *Dollars and Cents of Shopping Centers*, published by the Urban Land Institute (www.uli.org). Remember, however, that your retail tenant is not a shopping center tenant and has limited hours and market. The book covers 12 categories of sales, income, and expense data for 176 types of retail tenants. The information is based on confidential information collected from 1,000 shopping centers in the United States and Canada.

In addition, to counter the effects of inflation, tenants will want to adjust the breakpoint periodically. The CPI (Consumer Price Index) or other applicable index can be used to make such adjustments. Of course, the landlord will want similar protection against inflation by increasing the annual minimum rent by reference to the same index.

Breakpoint

A specified dollar amount of sales. A tenant may be required to pay a percentage of sales over the breakpoint amount.

Although some percentage rents are calculated using net sales or net profits, this method is generally not favored and is not the industry practice. The net sales method is more complicated to administer because of the additional calculations involved in reducing the tenant's gross sales by the tenant's business expenses. It can also lead to disputes about what are legitimate business expenses. Moreover, it does not reward either the landlord or the tenant for tenant improvements.

The following is an example of a percentage rent calculation.

Assume that you have entered into negotiations with a men's clothing store. Through research you determine that the average annual sales per square foot of a local chain specializing in men's wear is $150. The size of the sales area space is 1,500 square feet.

Multiply the annual sales per square foot by the sales area. This yields an anticipated annual sales of $225,000 (1,500 x $150 = $225,000). The annual base rent for the store is $20 per square foot, or $30,000 (1,500 square feet x $20 = $30,000).

Divide the annual rent by the estimated annual sales volume ($30,000 ÷ $225,000 = 13.33%) to obtain a percentage.

Therefore, the tenant will pay the landlord 13.33 percent of any sales over the $225,000. The tenant is given credit for the base rent before the landlord receives any additional rent.

If sales do not exceed $225,000—they total $200,000, for example—the percentage rent ($200,000 annual sales x 13.33% = $26,700 percentage rent) is not owed, because it is less than the base rent of $30,000.

As part of the percentage rent process, the tenant must report sales volume periodically to the landlord. The type of reporting and the frequency will depend on the type of retail tenant. For example, a package liquor store should be required to report monthly, whereas a jewelry store may report quarterly.

Regardless of the reporting systems used, an annual adjustment is usually made within 90 days of the end of any calendar year to offset certain months, such as December, when retail sales are traditionally higher, or January, when returns and exchanges are more numerous.

If additional percentage rent is due, the tenant is required to pay the additional amount within 30 days of billing.

What are the components of a percentage rent clause?

The percentage rent provision generally consists of at least six components. They are:

- definition of gross sales
- exclusions from gross sales
- figuring the percentage rent rate
- calculating and paying percentage rent
- tenant record keeping
- owner's method of verification

How are gross sales defined?

When defining gross sales, you will negotiate for a broad definition, while the tenant will want a restrictive definition. Generally, gross sales should include both cash and credit sales; charges for services, mail, telephone, and in-person orders; and deposits not refunded to purchasers. This definition may also include gift coupons, employee discounts, service charges imposed by credit card issuers, returned goods (especially when the measuring period is the calendar year and holiday returns occur in January), and bad debt on credit sales. In addition, if the retail tenant is part of a chain, the owner and tenant must agree on whether to include gross sales orders that are taken in one location but are filled elsewhere, as well as Internet sales. The location of merchandise exchanges can also be a problem if the chain tenant has more than one location. This can become an even bigger problem if sales are made over the Internet and returns are through local stores.

What are exclusions from gross sales?

Exclusions are items such as state sales taxes, item exchanges, trade fixtures sales, and returns of goods to manufacturers in exchange for purchase price refunds. If your tenant subleases some space through a licensing arrangement for a fee, make sure to include this "back door" income. You may want to include the licensee's gross sales as part of the tenant's gross sales, while the tenant will want to include only the license fee itself. Other exclusions the tenant may want to exclude as sales may include employee discount sales, fire or casualty sales, one-time bulk sales, loss leader sales, and mail order catalog sales.

How do I figure the percentage rent rate?

The percentage rent rate depends, in part, on the kind of merchandise and the volume of anticipated sales. For example, stores that sell food typically have high volume, low profit margins, and low gross sales percentage rates. By contrast, jewelry stores have high profit margins but low volume. Their percentage rate is usually higher than a store that sells food. To find out about the profit margins of various retail operations, ask a marketing consultant or your accountant.

FYI

Some percentage rent clauses can set different percentages for different goods, but do this only if you have the staff and time to audit the tenant's records. Another less onerous way of figuring the percentage is to use a sliding scale; that is, as the volume of sales increases, the percentage decreases.

When should percentage rent be calculated and paid?

From the tenant's perspective, the best time to calculate and pay percentage rent is at the conclusion of the fiscal year. An owner should rarely agree to this because of the cash flow burden a one-time annual payment would impose. The best advice is to make sure the lease calls for monthly payments of estimated percentage rent, even though this may place a heavy reporting burden on the tenant. You can compromise and agree to quarterly reporting and payment.

FYI

Calculating percentage rents for periods of less than one year can be problematic. In addition, some retail sales may be disproportionately high during the holiday season, thus a percentage rent calculation date during this time may distort the amount of percentage rent due from a tenant. These issues can be corrected by using projections of annual sales and then prorating rent monthly, or by using a calendar year adjustment instead of sticking to a lease year.

What kind of records should tenants keep when paying percentage rent?

All percentage rent clauses will establish requirements concerning the tenant's record keeping and the nature and timing of periodic reports to the owner. Typically, along with interim reports during the lease year, a final audited or certified sales report is required within 60 to 90 days after the end of the fiscal year. The tenant may want an expiration date for any claims by the owner of unpaid percentage rent, so the books can be closed.

What tenant records can a building owner audit?

A building owner should be able to examine records such as cash register totals, sales tax statements, and inventory sales receipts. The lease should state that if discrepancies occur that exceed a certain dollar figure, the tenant must pay the cost of the audit. In addition, the lease should state that repeated inaccuracies in the tenant's reporting constitute a lease default.

How do I handle retail CAM (common area maintenance) charges?

Maintenance services that are normally provided to an office tenant as part of the base rent may be performed by the retail tenant or paid for as a charge separate from the base rent. Retail tenants usually pay a part of the CAM costs of the building in addition to the base rent. All the costs of operating the common areas used by the retail tenants are added together and divided by the amount of square feet of retail space. If there is any vacancy, the owner pays the CAM charges for the vacant units. The CAM charges are usually limited to the common area that serves the retail tenants and their customers.

If the HVAC system is located in a central facility, the CAM charges will usually include a pro rata share of the cost of operating and maintaining that system. Other typical CAM charges include:

- janitorial cleaning of the retail common area
- window washing
- electrical cost of lighting the common area

- pro rata share of the building's insurance, property taxes, and water
- trash removal from a common collection point
- repair and maintenance of the common area
- cost of daily supplies and maintenance of any rest room facilities in the common area
- snow removal from the sidewalks

Pro rata share

The proportion of a cost pool the tenant pays when not occupying 100 percent of the space in a building.

What are exclusive-use and character-of-use provisions?

Under an exclusive-use provision, the owner agrees that no other tenant will use the building to sell competing items. A reciprocal lease provision, the character-of-use provision, restricts the tenant to the use specified in the exclusive-use provision. Some leases set a time limit on exclusive-use and character-of-use provisions or state that these provisions end when gross sales reach a certain level.

To maximize return on retail rents, especially if they are based on percentage of sales, both the tenant and the owner will want to ensure that retail tenants are not taking sales from each other. Lease provisions defining and restricting the kinds of businesses into which tenants can enter allow the owner to control the tenant mix.

FYI

Exclusive-use clauses can also cause for trouble when a tenant violates them. Sometimes strong retail tenants will resist this restriction to keep maximum retailing flexibility. The tenant may demand as broad a use clause as possible to accommodate changes in retailing strategy and to protect its flexibility. As the property manager, you want to achieve a balanced and diversified tenant mix and to avoid unmanaged, random assortments of goods and services that can hurt your retail tenants and potentially escalate into legal action.

What are continuous operation clauses?

A continuous operation clause requires the tenant to keep the space open for business during the term of the lease. This is an important lease clause because:

- A tenant may get a better deal in another building across the street and therefore want to lock up the old space so it cannot be leased to a competing store. By ceasing operations, yet continuing to pay the base rent (of a percentage rent lease), the tenant may stay in control of the space.
- In response to insufficient sales, a tenant may cease operations and payment of rent. Now the owner has to bring an eviction action, which is time consuming and may tie up the space during litigation.

To enforce a continuous operation clause, owners have three options.

- Remove the tenant because the lease is forfeited as a result of a violation of the continuous operation covenant.
- If the tenant scales back operations, ask a court to force the tenant to remain open through an injunction.
- Sue for compensatory or liquidated damages for lost rent and costs of re-leasing the space.

How do I negotiate signage?

Ordinarily, an owner and tenant establish in the lease the basic rules about how and where signage is to be permitted. Usually, an owner also prescribes specifications for signage along the facade of a tenant's retail establishment to regulate the size, materials, lighting, and even lettering the tenant is to use.

For the retail tenant, signage is advertising. More customers equal more sales and may result in a higher percentage rent to the owner.

Balancing the two goals of minimizing clutter and maximizing sales is often difficult. But it is better to avoid any later surprises by requiring the tenant to give details of all proposed signage, and for the owner to retain the right to approve it.

Specifically, you should:

- require the tenant to provide detailed drawings of all signage
- attach the drawings to the lease
- require the tenant to obtain all necessary permits
- if the signage is for a large tenant, such as a bank, make sure the owner retains the right (and the tenant pays) to remove the sign if the bank moves out of the building

Signage can take a number of different forms, including pole signs, signs attached to the front of the building, or signs posted on the inside windows of the store. Signs can also include banners, flags, and tethered helium balloons.

Signage must comply with the often detailed and specific land use, deed restrictions, and zoning requirements of the local jurisdiction of the building. These requirements, of course, override any lease terms negotiated between a landlord and tenant.

BOMI® INSTITUTE

The Practical Guide to Lease Administration

BUILDING OWNERS AND MANAGERS INSTITUTE

Lease Administration

Contents

Managing Tenant Improvements

Introduction

Lease administration is the process of fulfilling the terms and conditions in the lease contract. Once the lease elements are negotiated and the lease is signed, lease administration begins. This is a complex task that requires great attention to detail, and is one of the most important aspects of property management.

Lease administration responsibilities include:

- ✦ analysis of lease requirements
- ✦ collecting of rents
- ✦ maintaining letters of credit
- ✦ managing delinquencies and evictions
- ✦ enforcing miscellaneous lease provisions
- ✦ managing tenant retention and renewals
- ✦ managing tenant improvement allowances and project negotiations

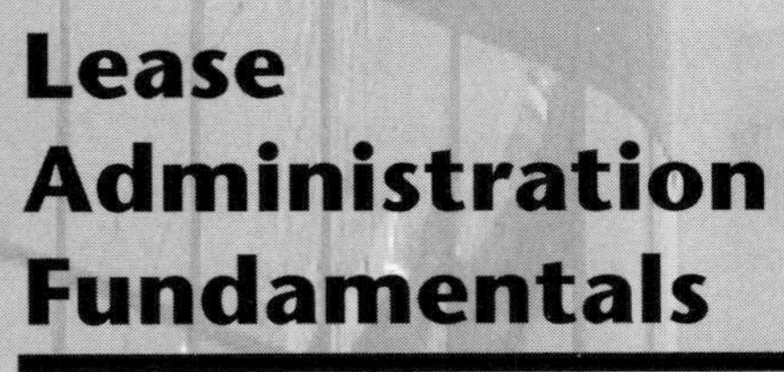

Lease Administration Fundamentals

What are the responsibilities of a lease administrator?

A lease administrator's responsibilities are critical to the financial success of real estate investments. Such activities include:

- enforcing insurance provisions
- collecting additional rents
- notifying tenants and/or owners of changing obligations
- renewing options
- reporting duties

In addition, a lease administrator will inevitably encounter breaches of lease conditions and rental delinquencies. The management of collections, delinquency workouts, and evictions is crucial to:

- maximizing investment cash flow
- avoiding lawsuits
- establishing a reputation for fair business practices

FYI

Lease abstracts and rent rolls summarize essential lease obligations. They also provide a format to compare lease rates and terms, and they facilitate property analysis and valuation. These abstracts also assist in the management of vacant building areas.

What are the four characteristics required in a contract?

To be enforceable, all contracts must have the following four characteristics:

1. The purpose of the agreement must be lawful.

2. The parties to the agreement must have legal capacity. (That is, contracting individuals must be at least eighteen years old, corporations or other groups must be legally constituted, and the parties must be legally competent, not judged insane or incompetent.)

3. There must be consideration by the parties in the form of monetary compensation, an exchange of goods or services, or some other good and valuable consideration.

4. There can have been no undue influence or coercion involved in the negotiation of the agreement.

Real estate contracts are also governed by the statute of frauds. Contracts for the purchase of real estate and conveyances of leasehold estates for a term of one year or longer must be in writing and properly executed.

What are the critical lease clause requirements?

Because a real estate lease is a contract, proper preparation of the lease is critical to property management. The following are the six essential requirements to create a valid lease:

1. **All parties to the lease must be completely identified**. Identify the owner or lessor precisely, and indicate the legal identity (individual, corporation, partnership, or other ownership form). In the case of corporations, indicate the state of incorporation. Identify the tenant or lessee in a similar manner, and include any trade names and an address of record.

2. **The leasehold (property) must be described**. Describe the leasehold in enough detail to eliminate confusion about the exact location and extent of the property. In the case of apartment leases, the postal address is sufficient to identify the location. In addition, include a lease covenant providing for tenant access to and use of parking and common areas such as:

   - walkways
   - stairs
   - laundries

- swimming pools
- clubhouses
- other amenities

Leases involving the use of land areas and improvements should include the legal description of the area. This should include the legal description of the property; the postal address, including any suite numbers that have been assigned; and a diagram of the leased area with respect to the property.

FYI

The use of the Standard Methods of Floor Measurement, ANSI (American National Standards Institute) regulation Z65.1, is one of the best methods to eliminate confusion about the location and extent of a leasehold.

Add a detailed description of any tenant improvements performed for the benefit of the tenant. Maintain as-built drawings for future reference and for updating changes, even though they are not part of the lease document.

3. **Consideration (payment or other compensation) for leasing the property must be fully disclosed**. The lease must detail the monthly or periodic rent and the total contract rent. The latter will be important if there is a default by the tenant requiring legal action. You can also include the annual contract rent for clarity. In addition, detail any additional rent agreements such as:

    - expense pass-through
    - percentage rent
    - CAM (common area maintenance) charges
    - insurance and tax stops
    - merchant's association and advertising charges
    - service charges, late charges, and delinquency interest
    - any miscellaneous charges that might be negotiated

Expense pass-through

A lease clause that requires a tenant to reimburse the landlord for expenses, such as insurance and taxes, beyond a fixed amount.

4. **The term of the lease must be fully described**. Provide the lease commencement date. If the exact commencement date cannot be determined when the lease is created, leave this area open by agreement within the lease and add by addendum later. Similarly, provide the termination date of the lease in the lease document or by addendum. Also disclose all extension options and requirements.

5. **The lease must include a description of permitted uses within the tenant area**. The permitted uses may be very broad, such as general offices, or may be narrowed to a single product, such as sewing machines. Permitted use clauses sometimes prohibit the same tenant from opening a similar location within a specified distance of the leasehold. Such restrictions may be a restraint of trade and are unenforceable as a result. Overly restricted uses are often violated by tenants and lead to friction between the landlord and tenant. Permitted use clauses can also cover lease conditions, such as concessionaires, lease assignments, and subletting.

6. **All other rights, obligations, special conditions, and privileges of both the landlord and tenant must be included within the body of the lease**. These conditions must be lawful and may not restrict either party in a way that is

prohibited by statute. These conditions include:

- quiet enjoyment
- restriction of antennas or loudspeakers
- maintenance
- insurance requirements
- surrender of premise
- legal expenses
- default and eviction
- assignment and subletting
- house rules
- a formula for cancellation of a lease in the event of condemnation

FYI

Samples of the critical lease clauses discussed above can be found in the BOMA (Building Owners and Managers Association) International publication *Office Building Lease Manual*. Some local laws require an attorney to prepare all leases. Even if this is not required, consult a qualified attorney before signing any lease agreement.

Although these six clause requirements are essential to a lease, there are many other issues typically addressed in a lease. Most additional lease language details the building owner's rights and formalizes the rights and remedies of the owner and the tenant in the event of a breach of lease terms by the other party.

What specific circumstances are often addressed in a lease?

There are many specific circumstances that either an owner or a tenant can address in a lease. These include:

- security
- parking assignment
- heating and cooling after hours
- communications antennas
- building names

What unusual circumstances can be addressed in a lease?

On occasion there are circumstances that are unique to a property that must be addressed in a lease. Some examples include:

- **The architecture and surroundings of an office building are unique to an area and closely identified with the owner**: The owner may therefore require a lease clause in all tenant leases stating that the tenant shall not use the image of the building for any purpose other than the tenant's business address and shall never use a picture or likeness of the building or premises in any advertisement, notice, or correspondence.
- **The construction of a project is dependent upon certain loan covenants**: The owner may require an escape clause to protect against actions by tenants if construction is derailed.
- **The building has glass store fronts**: A lease clause is sometimes used in retail leases to insulate an owner from responsibility for insuring glass store fronts.
- **A tenant has a boiler**: This situation requires a "Boiler and Machinery Insurance" clause in the lease.

FYI

An effective lease includes concise, clearly written paragraphs that cover each special circumstance negotiated by both parties. Do not hesitate to have clauses reviewed by an experienced attorney.

What is a relocation and substitute premises clause?

A relocation and substitute premises clause gives the building owner the ability to relocate smaller tenants to substitute premises to create larger blocks of space. This allows easy management of vacancies.

Sample Substitution of Premises Clause:

Substitution of Premises. Landlord hereby reserves the right from time to time to relocate Tenant to another part of the Building prior to or during the term of this Lease so long as the number of net rentable square feet so substituted approximately equals the number of net rentable square feet in the Premises, and Landlord shall not have any liability with respect to any such relocation and substitution. From and after the date of such relocation and substitution, the term "Premises" as used herein shall mean the substituted space in the Building, and Landlord and Tenant shall initial, date and attach to this Lease a substitute Exhibit A showing the new Premises. If such relocation occurs after Tenant has occupied the Premises, or any such substituted Premises, then Landlord shall bear the reasonable out-of-pocket expense of moving Tenant's furnishings and equipment from the occupied Premises to such substitute Premises and shall at Landlord's sole cost and expense improve the substituted Premises with improvements substantially similar in quality and scope to those located in the Premises then occupied by Tenant. Except as provided in this paragraph, all of the terms and conditions of this Lease shall remain in full force and effect with respect to the substitute Premises.

What is lease abstraction?

Lease abstraction is the process of summarizing critical information contained in a lease document. For efficiency, use a uniform lease abstraction form for each lease. Lease abstraction forms are generally designed to be used with a particular software or computer system. The following is an example of a lease abstract form.

Sample Lease Abstract Form

A) Property Name: Frontier Building
Property Number: 100
Tenant Suite No.: 802

B) Tenant Name: Fast Print Mailing Services
Notice Address: 100 West Main Street
Suite 802
Central City
Contact Name: President
Contact Phone No.: (362) 624-5413

C) Lease Term

From	To	Commencement Date
7/1/99	6/30/02	7/1/99

D) Security Deposit Amount $ N/A

E) Monthly Base Rent

Type of Space	Effective From	To	Sq. Ft.	Rent	Rate Per Sq.Ft.
Office	7/1/99	6/30/02	9,000	$15,000	$20.00

F) Additional Rent

Type	Prorated Percentage	Base Amount Index	Base Year/Date
Real Estate Tax	1.76%	$3,145,639	2000
Operating Expense	1.88%	N/A	N/A
CPI	30.00%	160.5	2000

G) Percentage Rent

Percentage Base
N/A

H) Parking

Spaces	Rate
4	$1,080

I) Options and Renewals

Effective Date	Rate	Term	Notice Dates
None			

Explanation of Items on Sample Abstract

A) The property number is a number assigned by accounting personnel. The property name and tenant suite number should be the same as the actual building information.

B) The notice address is generally the billing address. The contact name is the person to call to facilitate rent collection.

C) The lease term shows the length of the lease and the lease commencement date.

D) The security deposit amount should reflect only the amount of the security deposit paid or the amount of the Letter of Credit and expiration date.

E) The monthly base rent section should detail each monthly rental amount throughout the term of the lease. You may want to separately identify abatement periods.

F) The additional rent section should list all pertinent information associated with the tenant's additional rent obligations.

G) Percentage rent is primarily for retail tenants. This section should include all rate calculation information.

H) Parking shows the number of spaces and the monthly rate.

I) Options and renewals include term and notice dates.

This sample abstract form represents the minimum information that should be included in a lease abstract. Ideally, the abstract form should serve a dual function; it should make the abstracting process easy and support accounting and record keeping activities. The abstract form should be easy to read and understand, remind the reader of important clauses to review, and mirror the order of the information in the lease document.

What is a rent roll?

The rent roll is a quick reference for the basic lease terms of a building's tenancy. This document generally lists the important financial data for each tenant. You can use the rent roll to:

- verify monthly tenant statements
- monitor expirations
- answer tenant and owner questions

Every owner and manager has preferences about which items are included on a rent roll. The following example lists the more common items included on a typical rent roll.

Sample Rent Roll

Property Name: Frontier Building
Property Address: 100 West Main Street

As of ______________

Suite Number	Tenant Name/Contact	Square Feet		Monthly Rent	Rate Per S.F.	Lease Term	Lease Begin	Lease End
101	Workers National Bank	10,000	$	25,000.00	$30.00	10 yrs	6/1/97	5/31/07
102	Wahoo Steak House Joseph Sweeney	10,000	$	28,333.33	$34.00	10 yrs	4/1/99	3/31/09
103	Arrow Discount Drugs John E. Norwood - Legal Counsel	10,000	$	26,666.67	$32.00	10 yrs	7/1/98	6/30/08
200	National Insurance Co. V.A. Rist, President	80,000	$	133,333.33	$20.00	10 yrs	6/1/00	5/31/10
400	Lawyers Pension Fund C. Ira Crook, Exec. VP	24,000	$	42,000.00	$21.00	5 yrs	4/1/01	3/31/06
401	John Smith Real Estate, Inc. John Smith	5,000	$	8,333.33	$20.00	3 yrs	6/1/00	5/31/03
403	Norwood & Norwood John E. Norwood	11,000	$	16,500.00	$18.00	5 yrs	7/1/97	6/30/02
500	Continental Computers Chief Real Estate Officer	40,000	$	60,000.00	$18.00	10 yrs	5/1/99	4/30/09
600	Continental Computers Chief Real Estate Officer	80,000	$	133,333.33	$20.00	9 yrs	5/1/00	4/30/09
800	Vacant	9,000						
801	Vacant	16,000						
802	Fast Print Mailing Service	9,000	$	15,000.00	$20.00	3 yrs	7/1/99	6/30/02
803	Just Temporary Help Pamela E. Justice, President	6,000	$	10,000.00	$20.00	3 yrs	2/1/00	1/31/03
901	Pack Management Co., Inc.	14,000	$	24,500.00	$21.00	5 yrs	5/1/01	4/30/06
902	BOMI International	12,000	$	18,000.00	$18.00	5 yrs	5/1/98	4/30/03
903	Large Systems Specialists, Inc. John Stalick	9,000	$	13,500.00	$18.00	10 yrs	2/1/99	1/31/09
904	Vacant	5,000						
1000	BOMA Central City Chapter Executive VP BOMA	14,000	$	23,333.33	$20.00	5 yrs	4/1/00	3/31/05
1001	Byrne & Byrne Norvelle Byrne, CPA	26,000	$	47,666.67	$22.00	5 yrs	5/1/01	4/30/06
1300	Consolidated Telecom Real Estate Vice President	120,000	$	180,000.00	$18.00	10 yrs	8/1/97	7/31/07
	Totals	510,000	$	805,500.00				

Sample Rent Roll (continued)

Property Name: Frontier Building
Property Address: 100 West Main Street

As of ____________

Rent increases		Escalations								
Date	Amount	Prorata Share	Base Year	Tax	Op. Exp.	CPI	Security Deposit	Other & Storage	Parking	Renewal Options
6/1/02	$34.00	1.96%	1997	Yes	No	50%			$2,000	
4/1/04	$38.00	1.96%	1999	Yes	No	50%			$600	
7/1/03	$36.00	1.96%	1999	Yes	No	50%	$ 10,000	$200	$600	
6/1/05	$22.00	15.69%	2000	Yes	Yes	30%		$90	$8,000	2 - 5 yr
		4.71%	2001	Yes	Yes	100%				
		0.98%	1997	Yes	Yes	30%		$25	$2,000	
		2.16%	1997	Yes	Yes	No			$1,200	
5/1/04	$20.00	7.84%	1999	Yes	Yes	20%		$2,500	$8,000	1 - 10 yr
5/1/04	$22.00	15.69%	2000	Yes	Yes	20%				1 - 10 yr
		1.76%								
		3.14%								
		1.76%	2000	Yes	Yes	30%			$800	
		1.18%	1997	Yes	Yes	30%			$600	
		2.75%	2001	Yes	Yes	100%		$120	$2,000	
		2.35%	1998	Yes	Yes	30%			$1,200	
2/1/04	$20.00	1.76%	1999	Yes	Yes	30%			$800	
		0.98%								
		2.75%	2000	Yes	Yes	30%		$500	$1,600	
		5.10%	2001	Yes	Yes	100%			$2,400	
8/1/02	$20.00	23.53%	1997	Yes	Yes	No		$500	$10,000	1 - 5 yr
		100.01%					$ 10,000	$3,935	$41,800	

What are some other useful tenant reports?

Computerized databases can be used to generate several other useful tenant reports. These reports include the following:

- **Tenant roster**: The tenant roster is an alphabetical listing of current property tenants. When the contact name and telephone number are included, this can be a handy reference to facilitate rent collection and emergency calls.
- **Tenant profile**: The tenant profile is a printout of the data from the lease abstract. This can be used as an in-depth reference for more detailed lease analysis and to provide specific information required by an owner. (This report should be used for reference only. When dealing with tenant disputes, refer to the lease itself.)
- **Stepped rent report**: When you have leases that include rent steps or other scheduled increases, generate a report to alert the property manager of upcoming rent increases. The stepped rent report will insure that the computer billing information is correct and will allow you to communicate with the tenant about the upcoming increase.

- **Lease expiration report**: The lease expiration report lists each tenant's lease in the order of its expiration date—the most current expiration is first on the list. Review this report monthly to identify the leases expiring the following month, quarter, and year.

FYI

Tenant retention through lease renewal is an essential part of a leasing business. The renewal process should begin long before the tenant's lease is about to expire.

Remember that all of these reports are generated from a lease abstract and are, therefore, only a summary interpretation of each lease clause. Therefore, these reports should not be distributed to anyone without the written consent of the owner.

What are some rent collection techniques?

The following are several methods that can be used to increase the prompt rent payment:

- **Review rent requirements**: When the fully executed lease is delivered to a new tenant, review rental payment requirements and collection policies with the tenant or tenant's representative. At this early stage of the manager/tenant relationship, the tenant usually receptive to this clarification.
- **Diligent enforcement**: Enforce collection policies rigorously and with an even hand. Never attempt to bluff a tenant. Keep your word and be timely with collection efforts. A property manager or owner who is lax in collection practices will lose tenants' respect and other types of lease covenant violations will occur.
- **Monthly rent statements**: Send monthly rent statements to tenants. Although these are not required by all leases, tenants will usually pay promptly if a statement is received.
- **Change the past due date**: Consider changing the payment terms within the lease document. With the exception of governmental leases, rentals are paid in advance, due on the first day of each

month, and past due after the tenth of the month. Unless prohibited by state or local ordinance, rents could be made past due after the third or fifth day of the month by changing basic lease language.

- **Increase late payment charges**: Make delinquency more costly to the tenant. Within the scope of state/province usury laws, consider increasing late payment charges.
- **Hand deliver past due notices**: Whenever possible, give past due notices in person and call delinquent tenants about the status of their account. Keep these calls as cordial as possible, but insist that the lease terms are met.
- **Efficient collection**: Develop a reputation for efficient collection practices. Tenants will quickly learn that the property manager will use every professional and legal method to collect all rent. Never be vindictive or vengeful when collecting payment. But keep in mind that successful property operation is dependent on effective rent collection.

How should I handle insurance requirements?

Specific insurance requirements that should be addressed in a lease include:

- liability
- increase in fire insurance premiums
- fire legal liability
- workers' compensation
- business property coverage

Verify that insurance coverage is in effect at all times. Require a certificate of insurance from each tenant when initial possession is taken of the leasehold and each time that the insurance policy is renewed. These certificates will be provided without charge by insurance carriers, but often they must be requested by the property manager at the end of the policy term. To keep track of these expiration dates, generate a roster of insurance expirations from the tenant data base.

What are indemnity and save harmless clauses?

Indemnity and save harmless clauses require each tenant to carry liability insurance coverage and protect the property owner from unforeseen occurrences and tenant (or tenant employee or agent) negligence.

How should I handle additional rent?

Notify tenants of the amount and timing of additional rent liabilities. To reduce potential friction, provide as much notice as possible, with enough detail to show that the billing is correct. Remember that tenants have every right to examine the books that support your additional rent calculations and statement.

> ***FYI***
>
> **Sample lease clauses for additional rent charges such as percentage rents, CAM (common area maintenance) charges, and merchants' associations can be found in the BOMA (Building Owners and Managers Association) International publication *Office Building Lease Manual.***

How do I deal with options?

Options, such as the right of first refusal, are typically not difficult to administer. However, they are time sensitive. Therefore, having a computer automatically generate option notices is advantageous. If the current tenant does not respond to the option notice, a new tenant must be sought for the leasehold.

How do I maintain vacant space?

To maintain vacant space:

- Keep it clean and free of odd building components.
- Take steps to prevent or remove mold.
- Keep it free of odors caused by the growth of mold and mildew in dark, closed areas.
- Remove all of the previous tenant's improvements that are beyond reasonable repair. This will provide new tenants with a clean slate.

Vacancy is a reality for most owners and property managers. The presence of vacant building areas means that revenues are not being maximized. Vacant space can be very expensive because of both lost revenue and the fixed costs required to maintain such areas.

Vacant areas within a property are often small and scattered throughout the premises. Typically such spaces are suitable only for small, often undercapitalized firms that are a greater default risk than larger firms. Scattered, small spaces can seldom be leased to large or creditworthy tenants. Whenever possible, group vacancies together to facilitate leasing and make maintenance easy. Consider relocating existing tenants to manage vacancy.

Managing Tenants

How do I keep tenants happy?

To keep tenants happy, create a tenant satisfaction program. This program should do the following:

- **Deliver what was promised**: Make sure you know what was promised to the tenant in the lease, and deliver these promises.
- **Manage building staff**: As a property manager, you must create building management and maintenance policies and make sure your staff is functioning at an acceptable level.
- **Solicit feedback from tenants**: At the beginning of a lease and annually thereafter, use a tenant satisfaction survey to ask tenants what their needs are and if those needs are being met.

Sample Tenant Satisfaction Survey

L. Jones & Co. Property Management
Tenant Satisfaction Survey

Dear Tenant:

We strive to offer you the best services we can. To help us with this mission, please take a few moments to respond to the following questions so that we can better understand your needs.

Tenant:

Today's date:

Building name/suite #:

Tenant representative:

Length of tenant occupancy:

Management Office: Please comment on the level of professionalism and quality of action by building personnel. Are building personnel responsive when called on for assistance?

Maintenance & Cleaning: Are you satisfied with the quality of maintenance and cleaning service of tenant space, rest rooms, and lobby/common areas?

Elevators: Is elevator service within the building adequate?

Building Systems: Please comment on the quality of the building's heating, ventilation, and air conditioning systems.

Building Safety & Security: Are the quality and level of service related to security personnel and procedures adequate?

Amenities: Please comment on your level of satisfaction with the available building amenities (restaurants, shops, concierge services), and list any other amenities you would like to have.

Space Needs: Please tell us about any anticipated changes in your space needs.

Please share any other comments, suggestions, or concerns that you may have.

Thank you for your responses to our questions.

In addition, sponsor and spearhead building-wide programs. The following are some ways to improve customer service and create a sense of community in your building:

- Train security guards to be goodwill ambassadors.
- Loan out umbrellas with your company logo on them.
- Provide jumper cables and after-dark escorts.
- Offer concerts in outdoor common areas.
- Distribute a building newsletter.
- Sponsor a tenant anniversary breakfast.
- Send birthday cards to key contacts.
- Require your janitorial firm to meet with tenants every month.
- Send holiday gifts.
- Decorate on special occasions.
- Sponsor blood drives.
- Provide additional spaces for pregnant tenants and visitors.
- Establish tenant advisory boards.
- Provide high-quality HVAC and plumbing maintenance.
- Include engineers and mailroom personnel in programs.
- Sponsor book fairs.

(The previous list is credit to Trammell Crow executive Jon Dooley; *Software e-Briefing*, SS & C Technologies, Inc. 2003)

What are some typical tenant complaints?

In general, tenants' complaints fall into four main categories:

- **Cleaning**: Trash accumulating in elevators, halls, and other common areas can indicate that building ownership is attempting to cut back on expenses by increasing the cleaning cycles.
- **HVAC (heating, ventilating, and air conditioning)**: Building owners must spend the money to keep HVAC units in good condition. Improper heating and cooling in a building can quickly cause tenant complaints.
- **Elevators**: Tenants are often unsatisfied with the size, speed, and capacity of elevators, especially in older buildings. Poor elevator service is a common source of complaints.
- **Restrooms**: Be very careful when cutting costs associated with restrooms. Seemingly small adjustments, such as switching from paper hand towels to hot-air dryers, can be a huge source of tension between tenants and building ownership.

Remember that these types of issues are factors in a tenant's decision to renew or not renew a lease.

How do I handle service requests?

The best way to handle service requests is first to have a policy that explains how to deal with them. A written policy in the building's procedure manual can prevent a lot of headaches in the future. When writing this policy, make sure it is consistent with the owner's obligations under the lease.

A service request form is a useful tool that indicates:

- who made the request
- what the request is about
- who signed off on it when the work was satisfactorily completed

A service request form also allows management to create a database of requests and tenant contacts. This information can help managers identify service deficiencies and problem tenants and create new services where needed.

A first-person responsibility policy—the person taking the call sees it through to completion—can also be helpful. You can also require a supervisory-level person to follow up with a phone call or visit a few days after the request was received to see if the work was satisfactorily performed. Not only is this good for quality control purposes, it also shows the tenant that both the management and the building owner care.

FYI

Personality issues should never interfere with resolving tenant complaints and handling requests for service. Nevertheless, some tenants can bring out the worst in people. It is important to understand and recognize that these problems exist, and that one bad interaction can poison a well of goodwill. There is no one solution to this type of problem. Therefore, you must be sensitive to it, consider all the factors in each situation, and assign compatible people to each job.

How do I coordinate tenants?

In your role as tenant coordinator, you are responsible for:

- scheduling key dates
- getting the tenant moved in
- assuring that the tenant makes a smooth transition to the new space
- arranging for phone service and computer network installation
- checking on the quality of work being performed and the materials supplied
- scheduling freight elevators
- controlling costs and reconciling the job budget

The tenant coordinator typically enters the picture after the lease is signed. You will review the space plan with the tenant to confirm requirements. If the owner is doing the work under a work letter, help select paint and carpet colors. You will need to possess diplomacy and problem-solving skills. Your goal is to make the tenant happy while keeping expenses within the owner's TI allowance.

Once construction is under way, the tenant coordinator can become the construction manager and thus the owner's primary contact person for dealing with the construction contractor, its subcontractors, and their on-site superintendents. Above all, a coordinator must ensure that work is completed in a timely manner and tenants are moved in and able to start paying rent on the anticipated date.

What dates should I set for the tenant?

When commercial leases are negotiated, the tenant and owner usually agree on three key dates:

- **Occupancy date**: the date on which the tenant occupies the space to conduct business
- **Rent commencement date**: the date on which the tenant is obligated to begin paying rent in accordance with the terms of the lease
- **Lease commencement date**: the date on which all terms and conditions of the lease are in full force and effect

Keep in mind that the rent commencement date and the lease commencement date may not be the same. For example, as a concession, an owner may agree to a lease commencement date whereby the tenant occupies the space and must adhere to the terms and conditions of the lease, yet the rent commencement date may be later. See the sample tenant planning timeline on the next page.

	Week 1	Week 2	Week 3	Week 4	Week 5	Week 6	Week 7	Week 8	Week 9	Week 10
Lease Signing	■									
Space Plan		■								
Working Drawings			■							
Construction Bids				■						
Award Bids					■					
Tenant Buildout						■	■	■	■	
Letter to Tenant on Completion Date						■				
Move-In Procedures Sent								■		
Suite Punch-Out									■	
Keys Delivered									■	
Occupancy Date										■
Gift Sent										■
Lease Commencement Date										■

FYI

When negotiating a lease and determining the extent of the TI, it is crucial to consider the impact of timing on occupancy. For example, the length of time involved to construct a tenant space must be close to the dates for occupancy, rent commencement, and lease commencement. In most lease negotiations, the tenant is not obligated to occupy, pay rent, or abide by the terms and conditions of the lease until the tenant improvement process is complete.

How do I help a tenant move in?

Helping a tenant move in requires the three Cs:

- cooperation
- coordination
- communication

A fourth C, cash, is often needed to smooth out unanticipated problems. Make sure to keep some on hand for emergencies during a tenant move.

Early in the process, the tenant coordinator should arrange a meeting with the tenant's key management team to discuss the logistics of the move. The coordinator will be able to act as the go-between and, by working closely with the tenant's employees, can make the transition smooth. If the coordinator develops a good rapport with team members, it will be easier to find solutions when problems occur.

FYI

If a large company is relocating, there will be several different divisions to coordinate. Even though technically it is not your problem, your tenant coordinator should make sure all of the tenant's division managers are aware of the move-in procedures. There can never be too much coordination. Large organizations are notorious for the right hand not knowing what the left hand is doing.

How do I deal with lease renewals?

The process for renewing a lease is usually governed by a clause in the lease stating the terms and conditions for renewal.

The most important part of the renewal clause is the conditions under which the tenant must give the owner notice of intent (often three months to a year before the end of the lease) to exercise the option. This does not, however, prevent the owner from approaching the tenant prior to the stated dates to negotiate a renewal.

If the tenant fails to give proper written notice under the terms of the renewal clause, the owner may consider that the tenant waived the right of renewal.

FYI

The renewal option does not have to state what the rent payments will be, but it can contain language stating that the payments will be negotiated. If the rent amount is stated, then that is another concession to the tenant. If the rent is higher than the market rate at the time of renewal, then the tenant will not exercise this option. If the rent is below market, then the tenant will exercise the option, and you will lose the chance to increase the building's income and value.

Why is it usually cheaper for a building owner to retain a tenant?

The cost of finding a new tenant depends on the circumstances and market cycles. In a tight market, an owner can be selective and demanding. In a soft, or overbuilt, market, an owner cannot afford to lose tenants (unless they are not paying the rent).

Tenant retention in a soft market is important for many reasons, including the following:

- The space may sit empty and not yield rent for a long time.
- A long vacancy will affect the present tenants and their renewal negotiations.
- Considerable expense and effort is involved in marketing and advertising to find a replacement tenant.
- Free rent and other inducements may be required to secure another tenant.
- The current rental rate may be lower than the present one.
- The owner may have to pay to remodel the space to meet the specifications of the new tenant.
- The owner may be required to pay a brokerage commission.
- The new tenant may not be as reliable in paying the rent as the previous one.
- The new tenant's employees may create more wear and tear on the space and the common areas.

Why is it usually cheaper for a tenant to renew an existing lease?

It is usually cheaper for a tenant to renew an existing lease, because if they decide to move, they must:

- spend time to view new space with brokers and agents
- commit time and legal fees to negotiate a new lease
- oversee construction of improvements agreed to in the new lease
- coordinate the logistics of moving to minimize business disruption
- anticipate possible lowered employee morale, loss of key employees, loss in office production
- change the telephone system and all directory listings
- order new letterhead, envelopes, business cards, and brochures
- notify customers of the new location

All these drawbacks to moving may be irrelevant to the tenant if another building representative or broker offers a better deal. After all, this is a business, and price is a big part of the decision to move. Other factors influencing a tenant's decision to move may include the following:

- the tenant's dissatisfaction with building management
- the building's ability to fit the tenant's desired image
- the building's ability to meet the tenant's business needs

How and when should I renew a lease?

Despite any set deadlines in a lease, the decision of when, or even if, to renew a lease should be based on the strength of the market. Property managers should always keep their fingers on the pulse of the market and local conditions. There are three basic markets in commercial real estate.

- soft market
- traditional market
- tight market

How and when should I renew leases in a soft market?

In a soft, or overbuilt, market, the sooner you act to renew a lease, the better the chances of success. Don't wait for open discussions 30 days before the renewal date. In fact, many real estate experts say that you should approach the tenant before he or she approaches you—or before any brokers for competing buildings approach the tenant. By being first, you are also sending a signal that the tenant's business is important to you.

If the space was originally leased before the market turned soft, or during a free-rent period, the tenant is probably now paying a higher-than-market rent rate than he or she paid at the beginning. If you approach the tenant too soon, the tenant will want to negotiate a renewal—and reduced rent—before the lease expires to obtain immediate relief from its high rent. It could be difficult to pay the mortgage if rental rates drop.

If you are faced with this situation, respectfully (and tactfully) remind the tenant of the deal that was struck and the need for the tenant to fulfill the obligations under the current lease. Do not forget that the building's mortgage may carry certain stipulations against changing lease terms if they adversely affect cash flow.

Ideally, you should determine the best course of action by creating a spreadsheet that depicts all possible renewal scenarios. This data will help you to:

- decide the building's cash flow requirements
- forecast extended vacancies
- plan for brokerage commissions
- identify tenant finish costs

FYI

Renewing the lease of a cornerstone tenant during a soft market may be the most challenging assignment a property manager will ever undertake. To retain tenants, take a personal interest in their tenancy; act as personal liaison with the tenant, regularly make it clear you appreciate their business and want them to be satisfied. Provide excellent service, and respond to any concerns and/or shortcomings of the existing space.

How and when should I renew leases in a traditional market?

A traditional market will allow you to raise the rent when a lease expires, whether or not the tenant renews. When your vacancy rate is low, it may be to your advantage to let smaller tenants approach you about renewal. If the lease has been in effect for many years, the current market rate probably will be significantly higher than the rate the tenant is paying. If the tenant does not agree to renew, he or she will have to shop around for another lease in a market that has higher rates than they are used to paying.

How and when should I renew leases in a tight market?

If the market is tight and space is scarce, enjoy it while it lasts. Tenants will find it extremely difficult to find space that will be preferable to the space they occupy in your building, at the renewal price being offered. This situation will strengthen your negotiating position, thus freeing you from having to make any substantial improvements to the space or other significant concessions to secure the renewal. There's no downside should the tenant decide to leave. This marketplace calls for fewer concessions and requires lower tenant finish costs. The space will rent much faster and usually at a higher rental rate.

How do I determine the rental renewal rate?

Before determining the rental rate for the renewal lease, you must determine the costs involved in that renewal. To determine the costs:

- Ask the tenant what improvements the space requires, such as replacing the carpet or wall covering.
- Calculate the brokerage commissions that may be due on the renewal.
- Judge the condition of the marketplace, which is directly proportionate to the rental rate you should charge.

In both a soft market and a traditional market, your rent grid analysis and amortization calculations for tenant improvements will help you make a decision. These calculations may include additional factors such as the base rent of the initial lease. Setting a renewal rate, therefore, requires some homework.

Amortization

Periodic payments, usually level, which include repayment of principal and payment of interest in the declining principal balance of a loan.

If you know marketplace trends, you will have an idea of where the rental rates should be in the short term. For long-term leases, consider a lease with a CPI (Consumer Price Index) escalation. Rents do not always increase by more than the CPI, and in the long term, rents will depend on inflation and the local market. Even a stepped rate that starts at one level and is adjusted during the third year, the fifth year, and the seventh year of a ten-year lease does not guarantee that the lease rate will keep pace with the market.

FYI

One method of dealing with the uncertainty of future market rates is to allow an existing lease to lapse into a month-to-month tenancy, depending on the size of the tenant. This gives you flexibility, but there is nothing to prevent the tenant from giving you a 30-day notice of its intent to leave. With smaller tenants, especially those adjacent to larger tenants, this may not be a bad idea.

Some other trends to remember are:

- When the market is soft, it will have a poor absorption rate and declining rental rates.

- In a traditional market, consider the future short-term rental rate of the marketplace. If this rate has been increasing at a reasonably rapid pace, you may wish to set a slightly higher rate in anticipation of future rental rate changes, or you may wish to renew the lease for a shorter term.
- Pay attention to market cycles. Once rental rates have fallen in a soft market, there is a strong probability that rents will increase in the future. In a traditional marketplace, rents usually increase more quickly.
- Whatever the type of market, you may want to require that any refurbishment costs, except painting and cleanup, are added to the renewal base rent and amortized over the term of the lease. This will help keep the capital costs down because it gives the expense directly to the tenant.

Absorption rate

The rate at which space available for lease is taken off the market in a given geographic area.

How do I decide the length of a lease renewal?

During a soft market period, it is difficult to determine the length of the renewal lease. Again, the decision is based on the condition of the market and how quickly you believe that rental rates will increase. With this in mind, you should renew the leases of your smaller tenants for the short term and only if it is unavoidable. Renew the leases of your larger tenants for the long term.

Many tenants, especially the larger national ones, want to have a long renewal, but they will also want a way to get out of the lease. With many mergers and acquisitions taking place, expect the tenant to ask for a right to cancel at the end of a certain number of years. The penalty for cancellation can vary, based on the remaining lease term. For example, fees are higher for a tenant with a ten-year lease with a right to terminate after five years than for a tenant with a five-year lease with an option to terminate at the end of the third year. Some of the fees and charges to terminate may include one year of rent, unamortized lease expenses, and brokerage fees.

What is the difference between strong and weak tenants?

Every building has strong and weak tenants. Strong tenants:

- pay the rent on time
- expand their business
- grow financially

Weak tenants have the exact opposite characteristics. Appraisers believe there is a direct correlation between the value of the building and the strength of the tenants. Many people who purchase office buildings base their purchase price on this premise.

FYI

Stay aware of the business news affecting your tenants to learn their strengths and weaknesses. Monitor both *The Wall Street Journal* and local business papers. Plug in to back-channel networks by talking with tenants and employees.

Although retaining weak tenants does not enhance the value of the building in the long run, during a soft market, occupancy is very important. As a result, management must be flexible when it comes to rent-paying habits.

Even if a tenant with cash-flow problems doesn't pay rent until the latter part of the month, the tenant nevertheless ensures that the building has one less vacancy.

When the marketplace rates and occupancy levels increase, however, consider weeding out your weaker tenants and replacing them with tenants who want to expand.

How do I weed out weak tenants?

Weeding out weak tenants is simple: Don't offer them renewal options. In addition, make sure the original lease includes a holdover clause. A holdover clause basically says that if the tenant stays beyond the end of the lease, rent can be doubled or tripled.

If a weak tenant has a renewal option, say nothing. If the tenant forgets and fails to meet the notification deadline, then the lease expires at the end of its term.

FYI

Setting an unreasonably high renewal rent to try to weed out a weak tenant is a risky tactic. If the renewal option does not state the rental amount or a rent calculation formula, then unilaterally setting an unreasonably high renewal rent to force the tenant out may backfire in court. Judges have been known to rule with wide discretion, and you may lose on the grounds of fraud or discrimination.

How should I handle a tenant default?

All property managers will encounter tenants who are delinquent in their rental payments or who have seriously violated other lease covenants. These conditions are a default by the tenant which could make them subject to eviction proceedings. When tenant default happens, the owner and property manager have two options:

1. Negotiate a delinquency or default workout with the tenant.

2. Evict the tenant.

Under these circumstances the defaulting tenant has several options, including:

- Negotiate a delinquency or default workout with the owner.
- Accept the eviction and leave.
- Fight the eviction.
- File bankruptcy.

Most of these options are not particularly palatable to the property owner. There are steps that an owner can take to reduce bad debt exposure, but it is difficult to avoid it altogether.

What is a delinquency, or default workout, agreement?

A delinquency, or default workout, agreement is a formalized understanding of how and over what period of time the tenant will bring the rental account up-to-date. These agreements should:

- be in writing and signed by all parties to the agreement
- include a specific additional amount of rent to be paid each month
- detail how these payments will be applied to past due rentals, interest, service charges, and legal fees
- provide a specific date when the entire amount must be fully paid or the default condition corrected and any other terms must be fully met
- contain a journal entry of judgment for repossession of the leasehold property in the event that the tenant does not properly complete the agreement

When a tenant becomes delinquent there is a high probability that the rent will never be paid. Therefore many landlords think of a delinquent tenant as an evicted tenant. This attitude works well when rental space is scarce in a market area. However, in soft rental markets, an owner's cash flow prospects and reputation can be better served by being somewhat flexible when tenants are occasionally short of cash.

What is the Bankruptcy Code?

The Bankruptcy Code is a federal statute that, under certain circumstances, permits a person in debt to be relieved of his or her debts and contractual obligations.

Tenants can seek protection from creditors, including landlords, under the provisions of Chapters 11 or 13 of the U. S. Bankruptcy Code. All bankruptcies are heard in federal bankruptcy courts and are subject to uniform rules of procedure. These sections of the Bankruptcy Code allow tenants to reorganize their firms with the intent to make the firms profitable and satisfy creditor claims. Bankruptcy judges have wide discretionary powers when reorganizing firms.

A tenant in bankruptcy reorganization is liable for prompt payment of rents from the date of the bankruptcy filing forward but cannot be approached for payment of any delinquent rents prior to the filing. All past due rents become general, unsecured creditor obligations of the tenant, and full payment of these amounts is unlikely.

Bankruptcy judges are empowered to:

- alter lease terms and conditions
- permit the tenant to remain in the leasehold as long as current rent is paid
- repudiate the lease altogether within a specified period of time

Repudiate

To refuse to acknowledge or pay a debt.

If a tenant files for bankruptcy, it is imperative that the owner and property manager retain a qualified lawyer. Penalties for interfering with a tenant in bankruptcy can be severe and costly to defend.

How should I handle lease termination and eviction?

Terminating a lease and evicting a tenant is a process that involves a lot of legal issues for the owner. If eviction is done incorrectly, it can cause friction with a tenant who is still in possession of the premises. In addition, eviction carries expensive legal bills and possible lawsuits and counter-lawsuits. (This Practical Guide does not cover everything about evictions and should not be considered a legal handbook on the matter. Consult an experienced attorney for more information.)

Tenant eviction is a legal process. Uninformed owners sometimes evict tenants by locking them out of the space until the delinquent rent is paid. Such action constitutes a constructive eviction and produces a bailment for the sole benefit of the owner. Tenants who are locked out can seek civil relief against the owner, and the penalties imposed upon the owner can become very costly. Further, the tenant could claim that some business property is missing and make additional damage claims.

Bailment

Holding property for another person.

Proper eviction requires:

- actual notice to the tenant that it is in default under the lease terms
- a specified time within which the tenant must correct the default or face eviction
- a petition to the local court to order the tenant evicted from the leasehold

FYI

It is important to insure that your enforcement and handling of the lease agreement has been fair and neither vindictive nor vengeful. The tenant's property could be seized to satisfy a judgment, subject to prior lien interest. However, judgments will invariably prove very difficult or impossible to collect. The owner should not expect to recover anything beyond possession of the leasehold.

You should not try to do an eviction on your own. Speak with an attorney to learn more, because eviction laws differ by jurisdiction. Your building procedure manual should contain proper procedures for giving legal notices and managing evictions. Make sure, however, that these policies do not conflict with notice procedures set in tenant leases.

Although the property manager can handle many noncourtroom aspects of lease termination, eviction, and removal of a tenant, always seek the advice of a knowledgeable lawyer. If a tenant is not paying rent, you may need to address other issues, such as protecting the building ownership from becoming stuck in the quicksand of the tenant's bankruptcy and subsequent liquidation of assets.

What are grounds for eviction?

One of the clauses in a lease, often called the default clause, lists the various reasons a tenant can lose rights to the premises. This clause should detail default circumstances and lease termination procedures. Be aware that, when the landlord (owner or property manager) gives the tenant notice of the intent to terminate, the tenant has several options to remedy the default and remain in the building. These options are similarly outlined in the lease, including, for example, the option to pay all back rent due on the space. These default remedies may vary from lease to lease and state to state.

The following are some common reasons for default:

- A tenant does not pay rent or additional rent.
- A tenant breaks any of the terms, conditions, or covenants of the lease. (Rules for evicting a tenant for a non-rent default may differ from a rent default, so consult an attorney first.)
- A tenant or guarantor of the lease becomes insolvent or files for bankruptcy. (Be aware, however, that the bankruptcy code prohibits the filing for bankruptcy protection from constituting a default, yet this term is common in default clauses anyway.)

- A trustee is appointed over the tenant's property.
- The leasehold is abandoned.
- A tenant fails to occupy the premises after the lease is signed.
- The death of tenant or guarantor (usually if it is a sole proprietorship).

What is constructive eviction?

Constructive eviction occurs when the tenant is forced to vacate the space because the owner failed to meet the obligations and responsibilities detailed in the lease document. In a constructive eviction, the tenant cannot withhold rent until after he or she has moved out.

In some instances, a tenant who wants to get out of a lease will create a situation (like poking a hole in the roof to create a serious leak) and then claim constructive eviction. Therefore, you should investigate any constructive eviction claims fully. Don't hesitate to call in experts and ask for their written opinion, as well as any other documentation, about any suspicious situations.

What are the five stages of an eviction?

An eviction can be broken down into the following five stages:

1. The tenant goes into default by breaking one or more clauses in the lease.

2. The owner gives the tenant legal notice of default in accordance with the provisions of the lease (or applicable eviction law).

3. If cure rights are available to the tenant under the lease, the tenant fails to correct (or cure) the default after receiving notice.

4. The owner seeks legal judgment against the tenant to return the premises to the owner. By this time, most problem tenants have moved out.

5. If the tenant refuses to move, the owner recovers the premises with a court order and has the tenant and his or her property removed.

The eviction process usually begins at stage two (described above), when the property manager gives the tenant written default notice. A copy of this notice should also be given to the owner's attorney. If there is no cure by the time of the deadline, and the tenant has not moved out, the owner's attorney takes the copy of the notice to court and seeks a legal order giving possession of the property back to the owner.

It is important to know who should be served with any legal papers. Most leases state who is to accept legal papers for the tenant and who accepts legal papers for the landlord. In addition, the lease also states the office address for each party where service can be made. Depending on local laws, these types of notices can be served in person or by mail.

Before a judge will issue an order of possession, a hearing is usually scheduled. Next, the owner's attorney must send the tenant a notice of the requirement to appear in court, called a summons. The summons must be served in a specific prescribed legal manner. Attached to the summons is another document, called a complaint, that details the legal issues for the action. At this point, many tenants move out, making the hearing unnecessary.

Even if the tenant moves out, you must complete the eviction process. By doing so you:

- protect against a tenant's claim that it intended to remain in the space
- obtain legal authorization to remove any items left behind
- have the opportunity to pursue a money judgment

The tenant may decide to contest the eviction, which requires him or her to show up on the court date set by a court clerk. Once a court date is set, either party may seek adjournments, which may delay resolution of the matter for weeks or months. There may also be pretrial motions for discovery (seeking out the facts by going through your business records), which can include depositions (questioning under oath) of you or your staff. Your attorney may do the same to the tenant.

How do I mitigate damage from lost rent?

Whatever the amount you sue for, you cannot just leave the space vacant and let the losses continue to escalate. The amount of money you are awarded could depend on how you tried to mitigate (that is, reduce the impact of) the damage suffered from the lost rent. Mitigation is a legal issue that you should discuss with an attorney.

The best way to mitigate the damage from lost rent is to lease the space. This means you will need to make all of the usual marketing efforts and find a tenant that meets your criteria. In some situations, you may be stuck with having to take a weaker tenant and/or a lower rent.

If you evict a tenant for nonpayment of rent, you can also sue to collect the rent owed, plus legal and court costs. In some jurisdictions, the definition of rent owed is subject to interpretation. Is it all the rent and additional rent owed up to the time the tenant was evicted? Is it the entire amount of the rent obligation over the term of the lease (as described under an acceleration clause)? Or is it some other number?

How do I deal with criminal activities?

If you or your staff discover that an illegal activity, such as drug sales, gambling, prostitution, money laundering, or fraud, is taking place on the tenant's premises, your option for action is simple: Call the police.

Criminal activities are an obvious violation of the building rules and a breach of the terms of the lease. Refer these types of issues to the owner's attorney, who can also contact the police and institute appropriate eviction action.

What do I do after obtaining an order of possession?

After a judge issues you an order of possession, you can take the following actions:

- ✦ If the tenant has moved out, you may re-rent the space.
- ✦ If the tenant has moved out and left property, follow state and local laws regarding disposal of abandoned property.
- ✦ If the tenant refuses to leave, get a court order and have the appropriate law enforcement agency remove the tenant and his or her property.

How do I manage a tenant who is moving out?

The tenant must follow the building's rules when moving out. These rules can specify the times when the tenant can use the freight elevator and loading dock. If the move takes place after hours, the tenant may be required to pay a surcharge for building staff to be on hand to assist or supervise the move.

Inspect the space before and after the move to check for damage. Photograph any holes, rips, and other damage. These pictures may come in handy to support repair charges levied against the security deposit.

Make sure to get all the keys from the tenant, even though it is not critical to do so. As part of the move-out procedure, you should have the lock cylinders to the space removed and rekeyed as a security measure.

How do I deal with abandoned property?

In the event the tenant leaves property behind, don't throw it out before investigating the laws and the lease provisions regarding disposing of a tenant's belongings. Certain laws govern the disposition of abandoned property, and the former tenant could sue you if you don't follow them. In the state of New York, for example, an owner must obtain permission from the state comptroller before removing the tenant's property.

Depending on the jurisdiction, the laws may require you to:

- Create a written inventory of the property, and give proper notice to the former tenant of how and where he or she can obtain the belongings.
- Store the property until it can be disposed of. If the tenant does not claim it within a stipulated time period, the property must be sold if it is over a certain value.
- Place a public notice ad in a newspaper to announce the sale of the property beforehand. Proceeds from this sale (minus the owner's storage and advertising costs) may have to be given to a government agency for a set period of time. In some jurisdictions, if the tenant fails to claim the proceeds from the sale

after a year or so, the government agency holding the funds gets to keep them.

If a tenant moves out in the middle of the night and leaves equipment behind, your job now includes detective work. Before disposing of the equipment, as described above, find out if it is leased. This may require inspecting the equipment for any labels from a leasing company or calling the manufacturer with the machine's serial number to check for title ownership.

Managing Tenant Improvements

What is a TI (tenant improvement) allowance?

The TI allowance is the owner's contribution to putting the space in usable shape for a tenant's specific purposes. The TI allowance is the cost of labor and materials for construction and installation of floor finishes, studs and wallboard, drop ceilings, light fixtures, fire protection, doors, and various hardware and surface finishes.

Estimating a TI allowance so you can begin lease negotiations can become quite costly very quickly, before a lease is even signed. Your job is to keep the leasing process on track and the costs within reason. This is no small feat. To achieve this balance, you must juggle four tasks:

- lease negotiation
- space planning
- construction project management
- tenant coordination

In large real estate operations these roles are delegated. In small operations, you may have to do all four. But whatever your situation, keep TI under control by knowing your costs and your building.

Also, when considering TI allowances, consult with a tax expert because there are implications for tax planning and building financing. This subject is too complex to be covered here, but briefly, you must be aware of two key issues: ownership of the improvements and reporting the allowance as income.

What are the basics of TI negotiations?

Negotiating the TI allowance may begin during the first conversation with the prospective tenant, when he or she inquires about the space and rental terms. If the tenant pursues leasing your space, more detailed negotiations may follow. Such details may be delegated to specialists on either side of the negotiating table.

Failing to negotiate the TI allowance correctly could cause construction cost overruns and missed occupancy deadlines. These results can negatively affect the owner's budget, building financing, and perhaps even your job.

Make the TI allowance estimate part of your owner-approved leasing plan. This allowance can get a prospective tenant to indicate through a letter of intent that he or she is serious about leasing the space.

Besides negotiating how much to contribute in TI, you should also be prepared to discuss:

- the right to choose and manage contractors
- rent commencement and lease commencement dates
- the move-in date
- move-in coordination

In new construction, you will have to know the costs of finishing raw space. In an older building, much of the interior construction may already be in place; hence, the TI costs may be lower. Make sure to include demolition and debris removal costs if a prospect wants to consolidate several spaces in an older building. Renovation can become costly, because walls, wiring, plumbing, and HVAC ducts may need to be reconfigured.

What are the two kinds of TI?

The two basic kinds of TI are:

- **Standard fit out**: This is the fundamental finish package offered throughout the building. It includes a standard ceiling height in every office, standard-size doors, hardware, lighting, floor covering, and wall finish. An architect usually designs a standard fit out into the building at the time of original construction (or later renovation).
- **Over-standard fit out**: This is everything in addition to the standard fit out. For example, if a tenant wants 10-foot-high doors, and the standard door is 7 feet, the tenant should pay for the additional cost of a 10-foot door, plus the cost of changing the height of a drop ceiling to accommodate the doors if applicable. Be aware that tenants often ask for upgrades on the originally negotiated package. These are over-standard improvements and should be charged to the tenant.

It is important to note that as far as the owner is concerned, TI are items that are physically attached to the building and are thus the property of that building (depending on certain tax issues). Traditionally, furnishings and equipment, such as desks and computers, are not part of TI. They are the tenant's own expense.

How is a TI allowance paid?

A TI allowance can be paid in one of following three ways:

- **Fixed rate**: A fixed rate is a flat dollar rate per square foot that the owner contributes to the TI fit out. If the cost of the fit out is ultimately higher than the fixed rate, the tenant pays the difference. Using a flat rate method is the cleanest way to create an TI allowance because the owner does not have to estimate construction costs. Real estate professionals caution you to put limits on this allowance if costs come in under budget, because a tenant may want the right to apply any excess or unused TI allowance toward rent payments.
- **Fixed percentage or shared cost**: When using a fixed percentage or shared cost, the owner agrees to pay a percentage of the cost of the TI, usually with a cost cap.
- **Work letter**: A work letter is a detailed list of improvements the owner will make to the space. It covers construction specifications such as the types of materials and the finishes the tenant may choose from. Before using a work letter, you will need to know your construction costs. If the tenant wants over-standard work, get additional quotes. The owner can finance construction

above the standard materials by agreeing to amortize the improvements as additional rent over the term of the lease. Generally, however, most owners do not want to be in the financing business; they expect to be paid in one lump sum for any over-standard work.

How do I manage a TI build out?

For a TI build out to be successful, you must take these six essential steps:

1. Get a space plan drafted that is acceptable to you and the tenant. You can use this plan to do preliminary cost estimates and negotiate an acceptable TI allowance.

2. After you have a signed letter of intent, get professionally prepared construction documents (drawings, scopes of work, materials lists, and so forth) and final TI cost estimates. You will need these documents before lease signing because some will be attached to the lease as exhibits or addenda.

3. Invite at least three competent, respected contractors to bid on the work based on the construction documents.

4. Set a construction schedule and a tenant occupancy date for the space.

5. Keep tabs on the work as it progresses.

6. Coordinate tenant move in.

How do I obtain labor and materials estimates for TI?

To determine the amount of materials and labor your TI allowance will buy, you must enlist the help of a construction estimator. This individual (or company) is an expert at calculating takeoffs—construction industry jargon for measuring space—and then creating a cost estimate based on preliminary or final drawings.

If you are offering a flat rate TI, it is not critical for you to know construction costs because you are shifting the total costs to the tenant. If construction and finish expenses get out of control, it is the tenant who pays. No matter how you plan to pay for TI, before signing a lease, a tenant will usually ask for a firm idea of construction costs from an estimator.

Construction estimators can be:

- part of an architectural team
- employees of a contractor the owner uses for work in the building
- freelance
- from a firm that specializes in managing construction projects

Estimators may or may not be certified by professional organizations such as the American Society for Professional Estimators.

Estimators base their work on:

- ✦ knowing the local union or nonunion labor market
- ✦ sources and prices of materials
- ✦ delivery charges
- ✦ building permit costs
- ✦ other related charges relative to construction

They also use estimating data from commercial publishers such as R. S. Means (www.rsmeans.com) and F. W. Dodge (www.fwdodge.com). Dodge, for example, has a staff of 1,200 reporters throughout the United States who gather data on local construction projects and costs.

What is a space plan?

The space plan is the basis for the construction (or working) drawings, which provide all the elements and details necessary for the actual construction of the space. A detailed space plan shows dimensions and rentable and usable square feet. A space plan should include:

- clear room dimensions, with a scale
- a legend, which is helpful to read the plans
- well-defined work areas, with room delineations clearly marked
- illustrations of how the prospect's furniture and equipment will fit into the space
- plainly marked doors and windows
- a map showing where the space is located in relation to the core and elevator lobby

How should I choose a space planner?

If you're hiring the space planner, you need to look for the following:

- **Conflicts of interest**: The planner should not be handling competing buildings in the market.
- **Loyalty and confidentiality**: The planner should have a reputation for confidentiality, because many negotiations start well before anyone in the building or business community knows about a potential move.
- **Experience**: Space planners who have been in the business for some time have developed a reputation and have the knowledge to help you make a deal. They will be able to accentuate the features and design of your building through practical floor plans designed to meet tenant needs within a budget.
- **Quick turnaround**: In most lease negotiations, time is of the essence. A space planner who drags out the work can jeopardize the deal.
- **Enough staff**: Try to use a space planner who can provide one person who will service your account, but who also has a qualified backup. Make sure to learn how your project will be handled in the event the original planner is unavailable.

- **Understanding standard improvements**: The space planner should know what the standard improvements are and the impact over-standard costs may have on the outcome of lease negotiations.

If you are paying for the space planner, he or she is one of the most important members of your leasing team. Even if the tenant is paying the full cost, always remember that the planner has the ability to help close or kill a deal depending on his or her ability to work with you and the prospect. In other words, there is no room for personality clashes.

FYI

The space planner's ability to satisfy the prospect's needs while making use of some, or all, of the present office configuration is also highly valued. Reusing the existing features and finishes of an office space can save a tremendous amount of money and, therefore, allow the owner to offer the prospect a more competitive rental rate. This could also increase the odds that the prospect will become a tenant.

How can space planning help sell a prospective tenant?

One of the under-appreciated aspects of the space-planning process is the role it plays in selling the prospective tenant. Assuming that the prospect could select from among other buildings, use the space-planning process to persuade the prospect that building is distinguished from the competition. The more time the prospect invests in meeting with the space planner—imagining how the office will lay out or picking finishes—the more emotionally involved the prospect will become, and the more likely he or she will lease space in the building.

How do I integrate space planning into TI allowance negotiations?

The space plan is the core of TI allowance negotiations and construction planning. During the leasing process, either the building's space planner will meet with the tenant or the tenant's planner will meet with you to discuss how the space will be designed. The space planner can be an interior designer and is usually under the supervision of a licensed architect. This architect or architectural firm is ultimately responsible for ensuring that the final plans meet all building codes and other regulatory requirements.

You cannot begin to negotiate a TI allowance until you have a pretty firm idea of what the tenant wants the finished space to look like. Therefore, you must have a space plan to calculate an estimate. Commissioning an interior designer or an architect to design the space for the prospect's needs will cost money. But without some type of plans from these specialists, you cannot get an estimate; and without an estimate, you have nothing to negotiate.

Even if you spend money on plans, and an estimate does not guarantee that the prospect will sign the deal. One solution to this dilemma is to try to get the prospect to pay for any space planning. In addition, you can agree that the owner will reimburse the prospective tenant for a specific amount of money if a lease is signed. This condition can be made a part of the letter of intent, or as a separate agreement before signing the letter of intent. This is also one way to find out how serious the prospect is about the space.

If a potential tenant is willing to spend money on speculation, this is good evidence that the prospect is serious about the space and is not merely shopping around. As a general rule, however, prospects won't spend money unless there is a letter of intent or a signed lease.

Remember to:

- Allow time for extensive coordination, especially for complex projects.
- Be on guard at all times to make sure your TI allowance doesn't start increasing. (For example, the tenant's space planner may ask for a little bit more on the carpet allowance or a little bit more on wiring in a computer network). Make sure you recognize when the tenant's space planner is trying to add in additional items.
- Take notes at every meeting and on every phone conversation. Circulate these notes or a summary of the notes to all involved parties to make sure everyone agrees.

How do I manage construction projects?

A construction project manager must decide who does the construction and set a date for the tenant to move in. These tasks are usually performed while you are negotiating the TI allowance. All of these factors are integrated into the lease, often within a document called a work letter.

Since most aspects of TI take place in an occupied building, respect for the existing tenants and their businesses is paramount. This falls into the hands of the construction site supervisor, who is employed by the construction contractor. Loud radios, noisy subcontractors, and messy job sites are all nuisances to tenants, who may complain to the owner. Under extreme circumstances, tenants may even consider the disruption a constructive eviction, which may lead to lawsuits. Having control over the work in the building is essential, even if the tenant hires the contractor. Make sure you have a legal way to immediately halt work if it disrupts other tenants.

What construction documents do I need?

The complexity of the work and local building codes will indicate the construction documents you will need. These codes will also dictate whether or not the documents must be prepared and stamped by a licensed architect or professional engineer. In most cases, because of the commercial nature of the work, you will need building permits and formal plans. In general, permits are required for buildings being erected, constructed, enlarged, altered, repaired, moved, improved, removed, converted, or demolished. You do not usually need a permit for painting.

Construction documents include:

- scaled drawings that give the elements and details of the space and parameters for its construction
- separate mechanical, electrical, and plumbing plans
- specifications that clearly state finishes, construction code requirements, and details of the construction

> ***FYI***
>
> **Clean, clear construction drawings and specifications are necessary to obtain reliable construction cost estimates (takeoffs).**

How do I choose a contractor?

To ensure that the TI costs fall within the limits determined by the owner and / or tenant (depending on how the TI was negotiated), give construction bid packages, including drawings and material lists, to several contractors. The following is a sample TI proposal. The enclosures referenced at the bottom of the sample proposal can indicate either a breakdown of cost per construction division or a breakout of specific items that are important to the property manager for the project.

Sample TI Proposal

July 8, 2005

Mr. John James
Property Manager
Urban Real Estate
1 South Street
Baltimore, Maryland 21201

RE: BID PROPOSAL, TENANT IMPROVEMENT

Dear Mr. James:

We are pleased to present our proposal for performing the general construction of the referenced facility. Our proposal has been prepared in accordance with the following documents:

DRAWING	DATE	DRAWN BY
A-1 through A-11	4.08.02	ARCHITECTURAL FIRM
M-1 through M-7	4.17.02	MECHANICAL ENGINEER
E-1 through E-9	4.20.02	ELECTRICAL ENGINEER

This proposal is also based on the following clarifications and exclusions:

- All work is to be performed during normal working hours, 7:00 AM through 3:30 PM, Monday through Friday.
- The General Contracting Company, Inc. is to have free access to the site and all utilities at all times during the performance of this project.
- Tests and inspections, and their associated costs.
- This project will achieve substantial completion within TWELVE weeks of receipt of the building permit and executed contract.

The work, as outlined above, will be performed for: $**2,435,000**
Terms of payment: Net 10 days from date of invoice.

We appreciate the opportunity of presenting this proposal. Should you wish to proceed with this work, please indicate your acceptance by signing below and returning one copy of this proposal for our files. At your request a formal contract will be prepared, or we will review and execute a format of your choice. Should you have any questions, please do not hesitate to call.

Sincerely,
The General Contracting Company, Inc.

____
President

Enclosures

cc: file

Accepted By: ____________________________ Date ______________

FYI

Know when you must employ contractors who use union labor. In some cities, you may trigger a strike by unionized workers if nonunion construction labor is used in the building.

The person or company you choose as the construction contractor is responsible for:

- coordinating the subcontractors and assuring the owner that the space is built to specifications
- seeing to it that the project is finished on time
- securing lien releases from subcontractors and material suppliers
- completing punch list items

FYI

Your state and local building codes and professional regulatory agencies usually define qualifications and licensing requirements for building contractors. Look for a good reputation and a history of successful jobs when seeking candidates to bid your work.

On big jobs, you should run a credit check on the contractor and have the civil court docket checked by a title company to see if any lawsuits are pending over unpaid subcontractors, poor work, or other disputes. When selecting a construction contractor, consider the following traits:

- **Good reputation and references**: Look at work the contractor currently has under construction and talk to the client. Determine if the job looks organized and neat and verify the contractor's reliability.
- **Good subcontractor relationship**: If the contractor typically has good relationships with subcontractors, ensuring that their bills are paid on time and treating them fairly and honestly, subcontractors will be eager to work with the contractor.
- **Quick turnaround time**: Your contractor must be able to provide quick answers to questions and problems that arise, as well as to point out areas of potential cost concerns. When reviewing working drawings, the contractor might be able to make suggestions for saving money, as well as point out trouble spots which may cause delays.
- **Ability to perform accurate takeoffs**: The ability of the contractor to provide fast and accurate cost estimates makes

you credible with both your owner and the tenant, giving you a competitive advantage in the market. A contractor also doesn't want to make the mistake of underbidding the job based on its own poor estimates.

- **Compatibility with municipal officials**: A contractor frequently interacts with city officials and inspectors. A good working relationship with these authorities can make the job progress much faster. Likewise, a contractor who has many OSHA (Occupational Safety and Health Administration) citations for job site safety violations may cause the owner to be named as a defendant in injury lawsuits.
- **Integrity**: Past job references and subcontractors can provide insight into the integrity of the contractor you are evaluating.

How do I compare construction work bids?

When bidding out the work, always remember that the lowest price isn't always the best. While you need to consider a number of factors, remember that quality is remembered long after price is forgotten. After confirming that all other criteria can be met, find out if the contractor's pricing structure is competitive and realistic. By bidding out several different types of jobs (both large and small) with a variety of contractors, you can get a feel as to whether or not the prices are competitive. If the contractor gives you a lump-sum bid, ask for a detailed breakdown.

The three areas to watch are:

- labor
- cost of materials
- markup (overhead and profit)

What if the tenant will do the construction work?

If the tenant will do the construction work, the owner must have the right to:

- review and approve all plans and specifications
- approve all contractors and subcontractors for work over a certain dollar amount
- be indemnified against any liens
- require release of liens within 30 days after they are filed
- require proof of insurance (liability, workers' compensation)
- require all work to be coordinated with the building manager (such as the use of freight elevators and removing debris)

If you have negotiated the right of the tenant to choose the contractor, make sure to retain the right to hold the tenant responsible for all the contractor's actions. This is usually detailed in a work letter, which is also attached to the lease. Please refer to the Appendix at the end of this guide for a sample work letter/construction agreement.

FYI

If the tenant will do the construction work, make sure you get copies of all permits for the work. Also, specify in the lease that no liens will be filed against the building, and demand copies of all lien releases. Your attorney may suggest other rules regarding the owner's rights to control work performed by others.

What if the tenant manages the construction?

Either you or the tenant can manage the construction, depending on the situation. Each method has its advantages and disadvantages. When the tenant manages the construction, negotiates the contract, supervises the construction, and pays the contractor, the property manager has limited responsibility for ensuring that the construction documents conform to the plans. This reduces the owner's liability on quality or timing of construction, which can be a disadvantage if you want to get the tenant moved in quickly.

Under these circumstances, the owner may want to maintain some control to ensure that:

- construction is conforming to the plans and specifications
- liens are not filed against the property
- permits are obtained
- insurance is in place

How do I deal with a tenant who requests extra TI items?

Be wary of attempts by the tenant to get additional items not initially agreed to. If the owner is responsible for construction, your construction manager must possess diplomacy and problem-solving capabilities to negotiate with a tenant who requests extra items, such as:

- an additional outlet in an executive's office
- higher quality carpeting
- more expensive sink faucets
- different types of wall coverings

Any deviation from the original contract specifications should be made by a written change order signed by the owner. By creating a formal change order, you can try to keep the tenant from inching up too far on extras.

If the parties sign an agreement that change orders will add to the tenant's expense, make sure the tenant pays for those changes up front, rather than when the job is completed.

Change orders to the construction contract are generally used to:

- perform any work in addition to what was originally specified
- delete any work that is no longer required or has been given to another contractor
- rectify a condition that was unknown at the time of bidding (such as asbestos concealed behind a wall)

FYI

Whenever change orders are used, make a corresponding change in the final deadline for the project to accommodate the additional time necessary for implementing the change.

Appendix

Sample Work Letter/Construction Agreement

Exhibit to Lease Agreement between (Landlord) and (Tenant) dated ____________.

Tenant Improvements

I. Tenant Improvements Provided by Landlord.

Landlord agrees to provide the following Tenant Improvements in the Premises:

A. Completed Public and/or Core Areas finished in accordance with plans and specifications for the Building.

B. Floor: Finished concrete prepared to receive floor covering. Floor loading capacities: ____________________ (________) pounds per ft² live load, ____________________ (________) pounds per ft² partitioned load or per ft² in non-partitioned areas.

C. Partitions:

1. ____________________ (________) lineal feet of Building Standard partitions. Building Standard partitions to be erected to the underside of the suspended ceiling. Finish to be ______________.

2. Core and perimeter wall painted.

D. Painting: Colors to be selected from Landlord's standard colors and not more than ______________ colors to be in any ____________ room.

E. Doors, Frames and Hardware: ____________________ interior Building Standard (dimension) (material) faced doors with Building Standard frames and hardware including latch sets, hinges and stops; __________________ exterior Building Standard doors with Building Standard hardware including locksets and closers.

F. Ceiling: Suspended __________________ acoustical mineral board panels. Ceiling height ____________________.

G. Lighting: ____________________ Building Standard recessed fluorescent light fixtures placed one fixture per ____________________ (__________) square feet.

H. Building Standard carpet and base throughout.

I. Building Standard blinds on all exterior windows above ground level.

J. Electrical: ________________________ Building Standard 120-outlets; ________________________ of 120-volt duplex outlets may be floor mounted with the balance wall mounted.

K. Telephone: Building Standard telephone outlets will be installed on the walls or in the floor. ________________________ of the telephone outlets may be floor mounted with the balance wall mounted.

L. Heating, Ventilating, and Air Conditioning: A complete year-round air-conditioning system will be provided, including ducted supply distribution and plenum return air. The Building Standard mechanical system is designed to accommodate heating loads generated by lights and equipment up to an average of ________________________ (__________) watts per square foot. If Tenant's design or use of the Premises in heating loads averaging in excess of ________________________ (__________) watts per square foot or the re-quirement for special cooling or ventilation equipment (e.g., data processing areas, machine rooms and conference rooms), then the cost of any additional mechanical equipment or control required to handle such excess or special requirement shall be part of the cost borne by Tenant pursuant to Paragraph II of this Exhibit.

M. Plumbing: Men's rest rooms, women's rest rooms and drinking fountains installed in accordance with the plans and specifications for the Building.

N. Fire Sprinklers: Provided throughout in accordance with __________________ Bureau of Building requirements. Landlord shall not give credits for Tenant Improvements provided by Landlord listed in this ________________________ Paragraph of Exhibit __________ not utilized by Tenant.

II. Improvements Provided at Tenant's Expense.

All improvements constructed in the Premises which are in addition to the Tenant Improvements listed in Paragraph I of this Exhibit _________ shall be approved by Landlord and the cost thereof shall be paid by Tenant.

III. Design of Tenant Improvements.

Tenants shall retain the services of a qualified office planner, approved by Landlord, to prepare the necessary drawings including, without limitation, Basic Plans and Final Plans as described below (Tenant's Plans) for construction of the Tenant Improvements. All Tenant's Plans shall be subject to approval of Landlord.

Tenant's office planner shall determine that the work shown on Tenant's Plans is compatible with the basic building plans and that necessary basic building modifications are included in Tenant's Plans. Such modification shall be subject to Landlord's approval and the cost thereof shall be paid by Tenant.

On or before the indicated dates, Tenant shall supply Landlord with one reproducible copy and one black line print of the following Tenant Plans:

A. Basic Plan Delivery Date:________________________________

1. The Basic Plan due on this date shall include architectural floor plans, which shall be fully dimensioned floor plans showing partition layout and identifying each office with an office and door number. The Basic Plans must clearly identify and locate equipment requiring special plumbing or mechanical systems, areas subject to above-normal loads, special openings in the floor, and other major or special features.

2. Electrical Outlets: Fully dimensional plans locating telephone and electrical receptacles, copier outlets, and other items requiring electrical power. For special conditions, power requirements and manufacturer's model numbers must be included.

3. Reflecting Ceiling Plan: Lighting layout must be provided showing locations of all light fixtures and partitions.

B. After Receipt of Basic Plans.

1. Landlord's office planner shall produce full working drawings for instruction from the Basic Plan.

2. Landlord's engineers shall prepare plumbing, electrical, heating, air conditioning, and structural plans for Tenant's improvements and shall deliver same to Landlord for approval no later than two weeks prior to the Final Plans Delivery Date.

3. The preparation of working drawings by Landlord's office planner and engineers on the Building Standard Improvements listed in Paragraph I of this Exhibit shall be at Tenant's expense.

C. Final Plans Delivery.
Date:______________________________.
The Final Plans due on this date shall include:

1. Door and Hardware Schedules and Details: Complete details of doors, door jambs, and hardware for every door.

2. Construction Details: Details of stairs, wall and floor openings, and special equipment.

3. Cabinet Work Details: Details of all closet, paneling, trim bookcases, handrails, and shelving.

4. Room Finish and Color Schedule: Specification of type of wall finish and color.

5. Construction Notes and Specifications: Complete specifications for every item included.

Tenant shall be responsible for delays and additional costs in completion of Tenant's work caused by changes made to any of Tenant's Plans after the specified Plan Delivery Dates by inadequacies of plans and specifications or by delays in delivery of special materials requiring long lead times. Tenant shall further be responsible for such delays as provided in the Lease.

IV. Construction of Tenant Improvements.

A. Authorization to Proceed.
Upon completion of Tenant's Final Plans and at the request of Tenant, Landlord's contractor shall provide to the Tenant and to

Landlord the estimated cost of Improvements provided at Tenant's Expense pursuant to Paragraph II of this Exhibit ______________________. Within ______________________ (_______) days of receipt of such estimate, Tenant shall give Landlord written authorization to complete the Premises in accordance with such Final Plans. Tenant may in such authorization delete any or all such items of extra cost. In the absence of such written authorization, Landlord shall not be obligated to commence work on the Premises and Tenant shall not be obligated to commence work on the premises and Tenant shall be responsible for any costs due to any resulting delay in completion of the Premises and as provided in the Lease.

B. Payments.
Landlord's contractor shall complete the Tenant Improvements in accordance with Tenant's approved Final Plans. Tenant shall promptly pay for Improvements provided at Tenant's expense pursuant to Paragraph II of this Exhibit _______ upon receipt of monthly progress statements from Landlord, as prepared by Landlord's contractor, a sum equal to ___________ percent (_______%) of each monthly billing. Final billing shall be rendered and promptly payable upon acceptance of the Premises by Tenant in accordance with the terms of the Lease. Retainage pursuant to the terms of this Paragraph shall be payable with such final billing. In the event acceptance of the Premises by Tenant is subject to punchlist items provided in the Lease, retainage for punchlist items shall be payable upon completion of such punchlist items.

C. Final Plans Modifications.
If Tenant shall request any change, Tenant shall request such change in writing to Landlord and such request shall be accompanied by all plans and specifications necessary to show and explain changes from the approved Final Plans. After receiving this information, Landlord shall give Tenant a written estimate of the maximum cost of engineering and design services to prepare working drawings and incorporate the changes in accordance with such request. If Tenant approves such estimate in writing, Landlord shall have such working drawings prepared and Tenant shall promptly reimburse Landlord for the cost thereof not in excess of such estimate. Promptly upon completion of such working drawings, Landlord shall notify Tenant in writing of the cost, if any, which will be chargeable or credited

to Tenant for such change, addition or deletion. Tenant shall within ______________________ (______) days notify Landlord in writing to proceed with such change, addition or deletion. In the absence of such notice, Landlord shall proceed in accordance with the working drawings prepared pursuant to the previously approved Final Plans.

D. Improvements Constructed by Tenant.
If any work is to be performed in connection with Tenant Improvements on the Premises by Tenant or Tenant's contractor:

1. Such work shall proceed upon Landlord's written approval of (i) Tenant's contractor; (ii) public liability and property damage insurance carried by Tenant's contractor; and (iii) detailed plans and specifications for such work.

2. All work shall be done in conformity with a valid building permit when required, a copy of which shall be furnished to Landlord before such work is commenced. In any case, all such work shall be performed in accordance with all applicable governmental regulations. Notwithstanding any failure by Landlord to object to any such work, Landlord shall have no responsibility for tenant's failure to meet all applicable regulations.

3. All work by Tenant or Tenant's contractor shall be done with qualified personnel and in a manner acceptable to Landlord.

4. All work by Tenant or Tenant's contractor shall be scheduled through Landlord.

5. Tenant or Tenant's contractor shall arrange for necessary utility, hoisting and elevator service with Landlord's contractor and shall pay such reasonable charges for such services as may be charged by Landlord's contractor.

6. Tenant's entry to the Premises for any purpose including, without limitation, inspection, or performance of Tenant construction by Tenant's agents, prior to the Lease Commencement Date as specified in the Lease shall be subject to all the terms and conditions of the Lease except the payment of Rent. Tenant's entry shall mean entry by Tenant, its officers, contractors, licensees, agents, servants, employees, guests, invitees, or visitors.

7. Tenant shall promptly reimburse Landlord upon demand for any extra expense incurred by the Landlord by reason of faulty work done by Tenant or its contractors, or by reason of any delays caused by such work, or by reason of inadequate clean-up.

ACCEPTED:

TENANT		LANDLORD	
Name:	________________	Name:	________________
	________________		________________
Date:	________________	Date:	________________
	________________		________________
By:	________________	By:	________________
	________________		________________
Its:	________________	Its:	________________
	________________		________________

Index

D

U

V

W

Y